dubstep drumming

how to apply today's programmed grooves to the drumset

by donny gruendler

edited by rick mattingly

All music composed and programmed by
Donny Gruendler
Live drums recorded by
Donny Gruendler and Jace McDonald at Inc. Studios
Audio mixing and mastering by
Donny Gruendler
Illustrations by
Nick Casale at Casale Graphic Design
Photos of author by
Jon Hastings, Paper Submarine

*This book is dedicated to the memory of
Donald and Marilla Gruendler*

ISBN 978-1-4803-0534-2

HAL•LEONARD®
CORPORATION
7777 W. BLUEMOUND RD. P.O. BOX 13819 MILWAUKEE, WI 53213

In Australia Contact:
Hal Leonard Australia Pty. Ltd.
4 Lentara Court
Cheltenham, Victoria, 3192 Australia
Email: ausadmin@halleonard.com.au

Visit Hal Leonard Online at
www.halleonard.com

table of contents

preface

Since my background is in jazz, funk, and soul acoustic drumming, many students (and younger musicians) ask me how I became interested in dubstep. This is the story I share with them:

VERSATILITY TO WORK

Early on in my development I believed what all my mentors (and instructors) had told me: "If you are versatile, you'll always find work." As a result, I worked on swing tunes, shed my bossa nova groove, and whipped out the metronome to get my time together. I even brought a pair of brushes for a ballad in jazz band class! I was going to be versatile and become a gigging musician one day. Thus, I went through my high school and college years focusing on these broad musical styles. Versatility was the key to my success.

As I graduated from college and grew into a professional musician, I assumed (because of these formative years) that I was versatile enough to handle any playing (or recording) situation. I went on quite a few years thinking this way, too! I played small clubs with local top-40 bands, theatres with well-known jazz and blues artists, and eventually some stadiums with rockers. However (in the early 2000s), I got caught off guard when retro-DJ-esque funky artists such as Rick Holmstrom, DJ Logic, and John Medeski asked me to program loops in the studio, as well as trigger loops and samples on stage. I wanted these gigs, but I had no idea how to accomplish these tasks! Thus, I researched the DJ culture of crate digging, purchased an MPC (actually many MPCs), and endlessly read product manuals and forums. (An MPC, aka MIDI Production Center, is a famous drum machine made by Akai—see page 14). After securing the aforementioned gigs, I integrated these loops and samples into my drumkit and reviewed nightly gig tapes on the tour bus.

CONTRIBUTIONS

As I moved from project to project, I soon found that I also enjoyed the musical challenges associated with programming and performing with beat boxes and trigger pads. I was contributing to the music in a far greater capacity by providing additional non-acoustic drumkit textures. These ranged from keyboard stabs and full string-section loops to alternating snare samples within a verse and a chorus. Consequently, I sought out artists that utilized these modern sounds and began to work with them on a more frequent basis. In essence, it had become my passion, and I became known as a looping and backing material specialist. As time passed, I also realized that, prior to these working situations, I had ignored the integration of electronics within music altogether, which also led to me to stray from the traditional four-piece rock/pop act. Don't get me wrong; these styles are amazing, but I wanted to push my musical knowledge, producing, and performance style forward.

ELECTRO-HERITAGE

Once this realization occurred, I immediately began to study the historical lineage of electronic music. Just as I had traced the evolution of Dixieland, swing blues, and jazz in college, I followed Jamaican dub through to hip-hop, house, techno, UK garage, garage 2-step, and many more before landing on today's dubstep tracks. Just as in more traditional styles, each artist borrowed from the previous generation, in both harmonic and rhythmic vocabulary. In addition, each new development was also linked to advancements in technology, which was extremely reminiscent of rock and roll's journey (i.e., its debt owed to the electric guitar and the transformation from 2-track to 24-channel recording). As such, my spiritual connection to this music began to resemble that of any other, for the reason that real flesh-and-blood humans, who were pushing the envelope of their art form forward, created these languages and traditions. Electronic music had traceable roots and a deep musical lineage. I was hooked.

Over the years, I spent time solidifying the R&B, soul, and funk patterns of my youth alongside the jittered, chopped, and sometimes stiff sounds of electronic music. I was connecting cognitive brain bridges between all the styles I had learned. Once I had accomplished this, I felt like I truly understood music's (and especially drumming's) history and building blocks. To put it even more clearly— in my mind—I was able to relate an early Buddy Rich style drumkit to an MPC 3000, Apple laptop, and Native Instruments Maschine. They were all descendants of rhythm, beat, and groove within 20th (and now 21st) century popular music.

CURRENT TEACHING

I now preach that electronic music, computer technology, and an acoustic drumkit should coexist together. Not only did this lead me to become a faculty member at Musicians Institute (PIT) in Hollywood, California, but I am now their Vice President of Instruction and Curricular Development. During my time here, I've edited and created the curriculum for many classes. On the drum front, these include: Digital Drumming: Performance, Digital Drumming: Programming, Rhythm Section Workshop, and Dubstep Drumming.

In the end, it was the coffee-filled late nights, road notes, touring experiences, practice sessions, YouTube searches, and Spotify account that spawned many of the concepts in this book. I hope that you enjoy reading it as much as I enjoyed writing it!

Donny Gruendler

acknowledgments

MY FAMILY AND FRIENDS

Thanks to my incredible wife, Hope, for her love, support, and friendship; my son DeeGee for his immense joy and inspiration; my Gram for all of her support over the years; Bob Terry for his friendship, support, and countless hours of advice; John and Esther Good for their love, friendship, and huge meals; Rhett Frazier, my musical brother-in-arms and confidant; Rick Holmstrom for allowing me to experiment with technology on a countless number of gigs; the church of "Monday Night Football"; *Mr. Inspiration* Casey Scheuerell; Charles Chemery; the percussion staff at Berklee College of Music; all my colleagues at Musicians Institute; Mike Dawson; Theseus Montgomery; CAO Brazillia; Reginald Bloomfield; Jace McDonald; Jesse Stern; A-Ski; Kirk Fletcher; Bobby Tsukamoto; MPCs; 6-lug; Yamaha's Piano Black lacquer and Loud Series; Little-Airplane-Bottles-O-S; Mike Hoff for his immense support (so early on in my career); Joe Bergamini for always having my back; Sandy Feldstein (I miss you every day); Russ Miller; Stewart Jean; John "J.R." Robinson; Jon Clayden for always challenging me to deliver; Jose Ferro (aka the quarter note); Denny Freeman; Derek Jones; Chuck Silverman; Dee-Troyt; Versa Manos for my "doctorate"; Christian Lundberg; Coko Johnson; Joe Tamel, aka "tweaks," for helping with everything; Jon Hastings at Paper Submarine; Nov; Garrison; Hank Greenburg; Megatron; and everyone who has helped, inspired, or put up with me through the years. My composing, programming, and drumming are dedicated to the memory of my parents, Donald and Marilla Gruendler.

THE FINE COMPANIES THAT HAVE SUPPORTED ME THROUGH THE YEARS

Vic Firth Inc.: Joe Testa, Ben Davies, Neil Larrivee, and Mark Wessels, for believing in (and supporting) me for all these years; **Yamaha Corporation of America:** John Wittman, Athan Billas, Dave Jewel, Greg Crane, and Daryl Anderson for the toughest (and best sounding) drums I have ever played; **Paiste America Inc.:** Kelly Paiste, Andrew Shreve, Tim Shahady, Arturo Gil, and Jace McDonald for all their time, support, and wonderfully articulate cymbals; **Remo Inc.:** Bruce Jacoby for his support and friendship; **Steinberg North America:** Brian McGovern and Robert Sermeño; **Yamaha DTX:** *My main man* Bob Terry; **EV microphones:** Guy Low; **Ableton:** Dave Hillel, Cole Goughary, and Dennis DeSantis; **Modern Drummer:** Mike Dawson, Bob Berenson, Adam Budofsky, Billy Amendola, and Tracey Kearns for always including me in their magazine and initiatives; **FXpansion:** Clare O'Brien; **XLN Audio:** Andy Simon and Leo Der Stepanians; **Native Instruments:** Vince La Duca and Megan Griffin; **Hal Leonard Corporation:** Jeff Schroedl and the entire HL staff for making this project a reality.

about the author

Donny Gruendler was born and raised in the diverse musical surroundings of Detroit, Michigan. As a result, he grew up alongside an unusually broad range of influences including soul, funk, pop, hip-hop, traditional swing, hard bop, techno, house, and blues.

At age twenty, Gruendler graduated from Berklee College of Music with a Bachelor of Music degree. At age 21, he earned his Master of Music degree from Wayne State University in Detroit, Mich. Now living in Los Angeles, Gruendler has performed, programmed, toured, and recorded behind such artists as Kenny Burrell, John Medeski, D.J. Logic, the Funk Brothers, D.J A-Ski (Unique 74), Rick Holmstrom, and Kirk Fletcher. He has composed and/or played on jingles for Axe Body Spray, RE/MAX on the Boulevard, and NPR. His film/TV credits include *Last Holiday*, *Father of Invention*, and the Showtime feature *Chicago Overcoat*. Donny is also a noted producer under the pseudonym Inc and one half of the funky-soul-electro duo Rhett Frazier Inc. Okayplayer describes their productions as cosmic brilliance delivered via a well-stirred pot of soul, jazz, rock, funk, and gospel.

In the education realm, Gruendler is Vice President of Instruction and Curricular Development at Musicians Institute in Hollywood, California, and he is also a member of the *Modern Drummer* education team and a frequent columnist for the magazine. Donny has also released many instructional books, DVDs, and online content under his own name. For more information, please visit **www. donnygruendler.com**

overview

EXPLANATION

Unless you have only been watching reruns for the past few years, you probably have heard dubstep (whether you were aware of it or not). Dubstep is a genre of electronic dance music known for its head-nodding beats, dark atmosphere, and ear-shaking bass. It draws upon many other genres including Jamaican dub, hip-hop, jungle, drum-and-bass, and 2-step while fusing them into its own unique blend. Although it originated in the UK, dubstep is becoming a popular form of production (and remix) for the mainstream U.S. radio, TV, and club scene. Dubstep's main drumming hallmarks are rigid half-time beats, straight sixteenth to sextuplet rhythmic hi-hat permutations, and wobble-bass, all of which play off hard-edged synth melodies.

With these realities in mind, today's biggest pop, club, and hip-hop acts are beginning to use dubstep production textures to augment their stage performances. Thus, many acoustic drummers are also being asked to create these grooves, rewinds, and drops on their acoustic kits. Therefore, today's cutting-edge drummers are no longer ignoring *the trend:* dubstep and its textures are here to stay. Rather than letting DJs, producers, and their laptop rigs get all the gigs, today's drummers are emulating, embracing, and borrowing from them.

This text is a comprehensive study on how to play today's most popular dubstep grooves, winding hi-hat patterns, and DJ-esque delays on an acoustic drumkit. This will be accomplished through:

- A historical overview of dubstep and its related genres.
- Clear drumset-based demonstrations, exercises, and practice methods that are designed to help you replicate these grooves quickly (and efficiently).
- Detailed acoustic kit setups.
- A comprehensive list of dubstep groove transcriptions.
- Full play-along charts and corresponding mp3s.

BASIC MUSICAL ASSUMPTIONS

It is assumed that anyone reading this material has a basic knowledge of note and rest values, including sixteenth notes, sixteenth-note triplets, and quarter-note triplets, as well as drumset reading, basic chart reading, and some level of coordinated independence. However, if you need any additional information on basic drum technique or reading, many fine books are available from Hal Leonard that can aid you in your studies.

WHAT IF YOU CANNOT READ MUSIC?

I certainly suggest that you find a reputable drum instructor in your area and take some lessons to remedy the situation. However, I realize that many who are reading this book do not have the resources to take lessons or do not have the time to attend those lessons. Therefore, you will have to intensify your conceptual and listening skills. This can be accomplished by seeking out the songs from within the transcription chapter and listening guide. Many of these titles are readily available on Youtube, iTunes, or Spotify.

PLAY-ALONG MEDIA

Each chapter contains practice and play-along backing media at a variety of tempos. These include wobble-bass lines, synth stabs, and pulsating percussion. They are located on the data portion of the CD and range from 90–150 bpm. Not only will these items help you to apply what you have learned in a fun manner, but they will also put each exercise into a musical context. In addition, you should work through the slower practice tempos before attempting their full performance play-along counterparts.

FORMAT: ORDER OF STUDY

Unlike many instructional books, the topics presented in this book are not mere recreations of stock grooves. Rather, each chapter (and corresponding exercise) presents genre-relevant material alongside myriad rhythmic options, which are meant to unlock your own creativity. However, the chapters do progress in order of difficulty, sequential phrases, and feels.

For example:

- **Historical influences**: the genres that preceded (and led to the development of) dubstep.
- **The history of dubstep**: a brief study that presents the chronological developments of (and influential artists within) the genre.
- **Preliminary exercises**: this area is sub-compartmentalized into quarter note, eighth note, sixteenth note, and quarter-note triplet grooves. Each chapter concludes with nondescript backing material for you to practice and apply said material. Many of these sections also present:
  - Hi-hat permutations;
  - Multiple snare drum textures;
  - Select kit modification techn iques.
  - **Transcriptions**: This section presents many of the genre's innovators and their grooves.
  - **Full play-along MP3s** (and PDF charts).

"TIME" TO GROOVE!

Now that we have established that playing with and learning about machine rhythms is a must, it is time to implement these ideas and slowly build your practice strategy. Don't be intimidated. It is important to realize that working with these tracks is very similar to playing with a metronome. It will be difficult at first; but with practice, grooving with these textures will become easier each day. Furthermore, wobble-bass and DJ textures can be more interesting and mentally stimulating because they also provide you with a number of musical subtleties to deal with, such as *feel, tone, and texture,* whereas a click only offers tempo information through a simple "beep."

NOTATION KEY

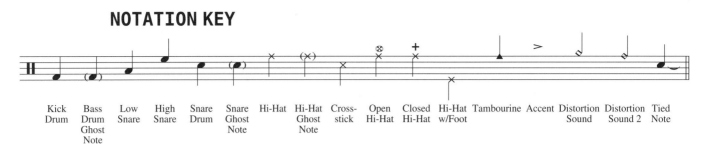

| Kick Drum | Bass Drum Ghost Note | Low Snare | High Snare | Snare Drum | Snare Ghost Note | Hi-Hat | Hi-Hat Ghost Note | Cross-stick | Open Hi-Hat | Closed Hi-Hat | Hi-Hat w/Foot | Tambourine | Accent | Distortion Sound | Distortion Sound 2 | Tied Note |

Double bar line: A double bar line signifies the end of a section or musical phrase.

Final bar line: A final bar line marks the end of a composition.

Start repeat sign/End repeat sign: Repeat signs indicate that a certain musical phrase will be repeated.

| Double Bar Line | Final Bar Line | Start Repeat | End Repeat |

Time slashes: Time slashes not only mark the beats of a measure, but they also indicate that a drummer plays "time" (i.e., grooves) as well.

Repeat previous bar: A sign indicating to repeat the previous measure

Multiple-bar repeat: A sign indicating that you must repeat a certain number of bars. There usually is a number above the symbol signifying the exact number of bars to be repeated.

| Time Slashes | Fill Markers | Repeat Previous Bar | Multiple-Bar Repeat |

Rehearsal letters: These are symbols that are used to identify certain sections within a chart. In addition, each letter usually represents a new idea, groove, and melodic motif. These can also be marked as sections, such as Intro and Riff.

$$\boxed{A} \quad \boxed{B} \quad \boxed{\text{Intro}} \quad \boxed{\text{Riff}}$$

D.C. (*da capo*): Return to the beginning of the chart.

D.C. al Fine: Again, D.C. signifies that you must return to the beginning of the chart. *Fine* is a musical term for "end." Thus, you will return to the beginning of the chart (D.C.) and end when you see the term Fine.

Tempo marking: This symbol indicates that there are a certain number of beats per minute (bpm). In addition, this is usually related to a specific note value. So, the example below indicates that a quarter note equals 102 bpm.

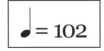

NOTATION INSIGHT

As you are reading through each groove example, keep in mind that the notated (written) grooves are the basic hypotheses of what to play. It would be quite impossible to notate every little "sound" or synthetic texture within a dubstep groove. Therefore (just like chart reading), it is open to interpretation.

QR CODES

Throughout the book, you will see small graphics like the one to the right. It is a QR code, which is a two-dimensional graphic that has a web address embedded within it. These codes will enable you to access (and listen to) the included transcriptions and additional content from your smart phone or tablet device. You can download free QR readers at both the Apple app store and Google Play.

THE INNOVATORS

While working through this book, you will notice that many chapters begin with a sketch of, and QR link to, an influential dubstep artist. Please take a moment to investigate these artists. Not only will this help you to relate to the music on an intellectual (and emotional) level, but it will also aid you in fully understanding each artist's approach within Chapter 8's transcriptions.

MORE THAN DRUMMING:
IT'S TIME TO TALK ABOUT MUSIC

It is extremely important that you do not think "drumistically" when working through each chapter, concept, or exercise. **This book is not only about drumming; it is also about *music*.** Musical sophistication, groove, feel, consistency, and comfort level take time to master. If you rush through the material and do not follow the proper methodologies—or just read through each section of this text—you will be defeating the purpose of your study.

AUDIO INTRODUCTION

chapter 1: influences

In order to fully understand dubstep's history, grooves, patterns, and textures, we must first take a look at the subgenres that led up (and contributed) to its development. This style was born from the more experimental releases of UK garage producers, who sought to incorporate elements of dub reggae, hip-hop, jungle, and drum-and-bass into the south London-based 2-step sound. Let's take a look at each subgenre in historical order and great detail.

DUB

Mid 1970s–early 1990s. Resurgence: late 2000s. 90–120 BPM

Dub is a subgenre of reggae music, which developed in the 1960s. Rather than employing live traditional reggae instrumentation, dub utilizes instrumental remixes of (and breaks within) existing recordings, which are manipulated and reshaped in various ways. First, the vocals are removed, which places a greater amount of emphasis on the drum and bass parts. Secondly, the rhythm section is then looped on tape (or between two turntables) to form an extended mix. Finally, extensive tape echo, spring reverb, dub siren, and the occasional "toasting" vocal were added to form a new composition. Thus, dub's pioneers treated the mixing desk, studio effects, and reel-to-reel tape decks as instruments in their own right, which began to blur the lines between engineer, DJ, and musician. In addition to a two-turntable setup, here are a few of dub's most famous tools:

toasting

Toasting is an early form of rapping, with heavily rhymed and alliterative lyrics. The performer using the microphone is referred to as the "DJ" or "deejay," and these newly created tracks are called DJ Versions. This was clearly the precursor to hip-hop MC'ing—i.e., the rapper and/or Master of Ceremonies.

tape echo

This device produces echo by recording incoming audio to a specifically spaced set of playback heads, which creates an individual repeat (echo). Oftentimes, these echoes degenerate in tone, so that each individual repeat can either become progressively brighter or darker as it travels through a mix. In addition, tape echo can also feed back upon itself, so it can also gradually build in volume as well.

spring reverb

Capturing the vibrations of a metal spring creates the iconic spooky dub spring-reverb sound. These reverb units are constructed by attaching a transducer to one end of a spring and an electronic signal pickup to the other. Due to their modest cost and small size, spring reverb units were widely used in semi-professional Jamaican recording studios.

dub siren

The dub siren is a very simple, hand-built synthesizer. It usually consists of a sweep-able oscillator and an LFO (for modulating pitch or volume). Dub artists use it to add spacey swoops and unusual FX type sounds to their vocal and instrumental tracks.

grooves

Dub utilizes three main reggae drum grooves:

one-drop

This is named after The Wailers' song (of the same name), and this groove shifts the snare cross-stick backbeat and kick drum to the third beat of the bar. Beat one is left empty, which allows for large, open rhythmic and melodic improvisations.

rocker

The rocker employs a half note kick drum pattern, which adds an accent on beat one to the traditional one-drop pattern. This groove was made famous by bass and drum pioneers Sly Dunbar and Robbie Shakespeare (aka Sly and Robbie). Various syncopations are added within both the cross-stick and hi-hat voices, too. Here is one such example:

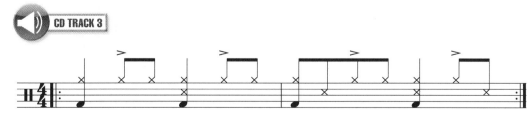

stepper

The stepper is a four-on-the-floor kick drum pattern that gives the music an insistent drive. Oftentimes, a snare drum rimshot is used in place of a normal reggae cross-stick articulation.

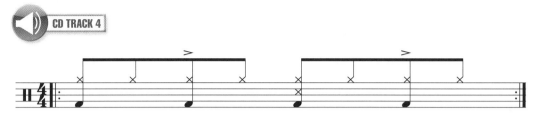

notable dub artists

Osbourne "King Tubby" Ruddock, Lee "Scratch" Perry, Adrian Sherwood, Mad Professor, Jah Shaka, Augusto Pablo, Dennis Bovell, and the well-known audio engineer Errol Thompson.

HIP–HOP

Mid 1970s–early 1990s. Resurgence: early 2000s. 85–98 BPM

Hip-hop is both music and culture. It formed in the 1970s during the many Bronx, New York block parties. Throughout these gatherings, DJs played many popular funk, disco, and soul recordings. In order to keep the dance floor moving, they isolated (and extended) the short drum breaks from within many of these songs. This was accomplished by implementing a two-turntable setup, which played two identical alternating records (and drum breaks) in order to form a continuous breakbeat/drum loop. This technique was borrowed from Jamaican dub music (and introduced to the U.S. by DJ Kool Herc, widely considered the father of hip-hop). Soon thereafter, scratching, beat matching, and beat juggling began to develop alongside these breaks. Altogether, this helped to form the hip-hop bed tracks that MCs rapped over.

In the mid 1980s, samplers such as the AKAI S900 and MPC 3000 began to replace the two-turntable setup. With these devices, the process of looping a break into a breakbeat became more common. Let's briefly take a look at hip-hop's main devices and famous breakbeats:

sampler

A sampler is an electronic musical instrument that is similar to a synthesizer. Instead of generating sounds, it uses recordings, or "samples," of sounds that are recorded into it by the user. The samples are played back by means of a keyboard, sequencer, or other triggering device. A single sample may often be pitch-shifted to produce musical scales and chords. Many samplers feature filters, modulation, low-frequency oscillation, and other synthesizer-like processes that allow the original sound to be modified in many different ways. The most famous sampler to many early DJs was the AKAI MPC 60.

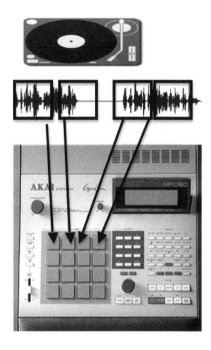

Akai's MPC is an acronym for MIDI Production Center. It is an "all-in-one" studio-quality sampler, drum machine, and sequencer built into one hardware unit. The MPC's strength is in its ability to mash up, deconstruct, and reassemble a breakbeat (or any sampled phrase) in a multitude of ways. Many producers would record a sample from vinyl, chop it into fragments, assign each chopped fragment-sample to a trigger pad, add effects, play it in real-time, and sequence it—all in this groove-box. (Right)

grooves

Hip-hop can employ a multitude of drum grooves. I have listed two stereotypical examples for you below:

eighth-note groove

Most early hip-hop grooves consisted of eighth notes and featured a wide synthetic reverb-gated snare on beats two and four.

eighth-note hi-hat with sixteenth kick

Later on, elongated clap sounds were used alongside both straight and shuffled sixteenth-note kick patterns.

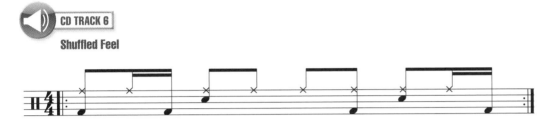

Early hip-hop artists utilized breakbeats or single drum samples to construct their drum grooves. It was not until the 1990s when artists began to use acoustic drummers such as Amir "Questlove" Thompson on their tracks.

notable hip-hop artists

Boogie Down Productions, KRS One, Dr. Dre, Run DMC, Eminem, Jay-Z, The Roots, and Big Daddy Kane.

JUNGLE

Early 1990s. Old Skool: 130–140 BPM; Modern: 155–165 BPM

Just as in hip-hop, the term jungle can also be traced to the lyrics used within Jamaican toasting. Numerous references to "jungle," "junglists," and "jungle music" are found throughout hundreds of dub, reggae, and dance tracks. Not only does this style incorporate the previously mentioned effects-based production elements and deep bass lines of Jamaican dub, but it also expands on them by incorporating up-tempo breakbeats and techno music textures. In addition, this style is universally known for its fast, syncopated, chopped, and rearranged drum patterns, which producers created by cutting up sampled breakbeats (most notably the Amen Break) on early 1980s Akai Samplers, MPCs and Atari ST computers. This process was very similar to hip-hop, but much more complex. In the early 1990s, these breaks were layered with long pitch-shifted snare rolls and Roland TR-808/909 bass drum sounds, which became synonymous with the jungle genre.

Amen Break

The Amen Break is a brief drum solo break within the 1969 song "Amen, Brother." Gregory Cylvester "G. C" Coleman performed it as a member of the Winstons (a popular 1960s funk-soul group). It gained worldwide fame in the 1980s, when four bars (5.2 seconds) of it was sampled, which ultimately formed the basis of many new compositions.

chopped and rearranged

Here is an example of how the Amen Break would be chopped, mangled, and rearranged with a sampler or MPC-style groove box:

layered samples and rolls added

Here is an example of how the previous chopped breakbeat would be layered alongside long pitch-shifted snare rolls, and Roland TR-808/909-style kick drum sounds.

notable jungle artists

Babylon Timewarp, DJ Hype, Congo Natty, Boogie Times Tribe, Shy FX, and a Guy Called Gerald.

DRUM-AND-BASS

Early–Mid 1990s. 160–180 BPM

By 1995, the term "jungle" was synonymous with the dub-influenced sound. Therefore, DJs (and producers) who did not incorporate reggae elements within their mixes began to adopt the term "drum-and-bass" (aka drum'n'bass). Sonically, drum-and-bass incorporated a much wider range of influences than jungle. These ranged from the highly electronic, industrial sounds of techno to the use of conventional, acoustic jazz-influenced instrumentation.

Just like jungle, drum-and-bass also relied heavily on syncopated drum programming, long pitched snare rolls, and Roland TR-808/909-style kick drum sounds. However, drum-and-bass sought to utilize the Amen Break in more intricate ways, such as smaller fragment chops, stutters, and the like. These more refined chops were placed alongside a simple synthesized atmospheric sounding track, which contrasted the very busy instrumentation of jungle.

Amen Break, drum-and-bass style

Here is an example of how the previous Amen-style break would be further refined, chopped, mangled, and rearranged within the drum-and-bass style. You'll notice the smaller subdivided chops, stutters, and restarts within the pattern.

notable drum-and-bass artists

Pendulum, SNAP!, Moguai, Roni Size, and Photek.

jungle vs. drum-and-bass

Currently, the difference between jungle and drum-and-bass is negligible; there is no universally accepted semantic distinction between the two. Thus, some DJs associate "jungle" with older material from the first half of the 1990s, which essentially precedes drum-and-bass. Others use jungle as shorthand for ragga jungle, a specific, small sub-genre within the broader realm of up-to-date drum-and-bass. However, most agree that these terms are synonymous and interchangeable.

GARAGE

Mid–late 1990s. 138–143 BPM

Garage was a descendant of house music, which originated in the U.S. cities of Chicago, Detroit, New Jersey, and New York. The original term (and musical direction of) garage was influenced by the four-on-the-floor rhythms from the New York-based 1980s discothèque Paradise Garage. Not only did this genre feature an incessant syncopated 4/4 rhythm, but it also had shuffled hi-hats and beat-skipping kick drums throughout. Garage tracks also commonly featured chopped up and pitch-shifted vocal samples that complement the underlying rhythmic structure. Later on in the UK, garage was played at jungle club events (within a second smaller room). In order for these tracks to be palatable to a jungle audience, DJs sped up these garage tracks to approximately 138 bpm. The media started to call this tempo-altered type of garage music "speed garage," which was 2-step's immediate predecessor.

grooves

Garage utilized traditional house grooves and the modern production techniques of jungle. Let's take a look at a typical house and garage groove:

house

Most house grooves consisted of both eighths and sixteenth notes and featured a four-on-the-floor kick alongside syncopated hi-hats:

UK garage

Later on, shorter snare sounds were used alongside sixteenth-note kick patterns. These were both straight and shuffled.

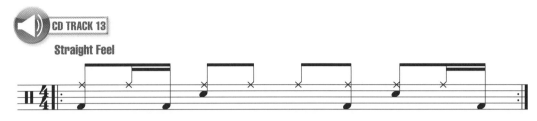

notable garage artists

Artful Dodger, So Solid Crew, Todd Edwards, Groove Chronicles, Ms Dynamite, and Oxide and Nuetrino.

2–STEP GARAGE

Mid-1990s–early 2000s. 136–145 BPM

2-step became popular as both an evolution of, and reaction to, the developments within jungle and speed garage. During their off-peak hours, many London-based jungle pirate radio stations played 2-step tracks. During these shows, the DJs mixed UK garage productions with American house and garage producers, while simultaneously (and collectively) pitching up the records to 130 bpm (the U.S. tempos mimicked the disco tempos, which ranged between 100–120 bpm). Soon, UK producers began to emulate the sound of these pitched-up, imported records within their own tracks, and this led to the full 2-step movement.

groove

A 2-step garage groove places the kick on beat one with syncopated percussion on the off-beats. It can be either shuffled or straight, and routinely features off-beat kick drums that alternate between low and high frequencies. Usually, the hi-hats are played on the upbeat to help propel the music forward.

notable 2–step garage artists

Burial, Katy B, Luck and Neat, and Zed Bias.

CULMINATION

Each of the previously mentioned genres had an impact on the production methods, sound, and overall vision that is dubstep. Thus, on the following pages, let's look at dubstep's evolution within each of the aforementioned styles in greater detail.

Chapter 2: A Brief History of Dubstep

While originating in the UK, dubstep is becoming a popular form of production within the mainstream U.S. radio, TV, and club scene. Dubstep's main hallmarks are rigid 2-step half-time beats, straight sixteenth rhythmic permutations, and most notably, deep sub-frequency "wobble-bass" (which we will cover in detail in the next section). Each of these traits plays off shrill (and hard-edged synth) melodies, which ultimately leave a gaping hole in the midrange frequencies. Altogether, this adds to dubstep's powerful and dark atmospheric minimalist style.

In addition, dubstep's moniker stems from a simple combination of genres: Jamaican **dub** music and the UK **2-step** rhythm. However, its exact roots (and historical timing) are a bit tougher to pinpoint, as this style is a collateral descendant of most (if not all) DJ cultures. As we have studied in the preceding pages, these also include (but are not limited to) hip-hop, jungle, drum-and-bass, garage, and 2-step. With this in mind, let's take a closer look at dubstep's heritage that spans from approximately 1999 to present day:

EARLY FORMATIONS

Dubstep's earliest inception dates back to 1999, when pioneer electronic 2-step artists such as El-B, Zed Bias, Steve Gurley, and Oris Jay began to experiment with a new, more innovative bass-heavy music. It was through their melodic explorations at the Ammunition Productions club entitled Forward>> that dubstep began to form. (Forward>> also featured artists who made forms of dark garage music, giving the collective scene the moniker "The Forward>> sound.")

Not only did this Soho London establishment allow their artists to experiment with subsonic sounds live on stage, but they also supported these artists by founding many early dubstep record labels including Tempa, Soulja, Road, Vehicle, Shelflife, Texture, Lifestyle, and Bingo. Concurrently, they also founded a pirate radio station, Rinse FM. Kode9, an early dubstep innovator himself, hosted a show on this station, which heavily promoted and played this new bass-heavy music. Altogether, the music that the Forward>> brand promoted was so different that an online flyer described its sound as "basslines to make your chest cavity shudder."

In 2002, the U.S. magazine *XLR8R* ran a cover story about this burgeoning new UK electronic music scene and the Forward>> culture. It featured the pioneering dubstep trio Horsepower Productions, and was titled "An inside look at London's dub 2-step underground." Within its pages, it affectionately called the new music style "dubstep." Soon thereafter, while paying tribute to this new terminology, the Tempa record label (founded by the aforementioned Ammunition Promotions) released *Dubstep Allstars Vol. 1* by DJ Hatcha.

Concurrently, a Croydon (South London) record store called Big Apple was infiltrating the electronic music community by stocking early UK hardcore, rave, techno, house, garage, and drum-and-bass music. They also created listening rooms for the public and employed early dubstep DJs (and producers) such as Skream and DJ Hatcha. Digital Mystikz, El-B, Zed Bias, Horsepower Productions, Plastician, N Type, Walsh, and a young Loefah were frequent visitors to the shop as well. Thereafter, this locale was synonymous with the latest dubstep releases. Altogether, these seemingly random occurrences solidified this new movement and established London as a safe haven for these up-and-coming artists (and listeners).

A FLOURISHING SCENE

In 2003, The UK up-tempo styles of jungle, 2-step, and garage were gaining popularity, which ultimately led to their sonic options (and tempos) becoming overused. In reaction to this trend, many of the aforementioned artists responded by creating slower, sinister, darker, and moodier electronic-based tracks. Concurrently, DJ Hatcha began to expand dubstep's dark, clipped, and minimal sound by playing his unreleased material via 10-inch dubplates on Rinse FM. (Dubplates are heavy-gauge test record pressings that are not made available to the public.) Soon thereafter, a weekly event at Forward>> titled "Filthy Dub" (founded by famed electronic artist Plastician) allowed influential DJs such as Skream, Benga, N Type, and Cyrus to make their official debuts.

It was around this time that Mala and Coki (together Digital Mystikz) started adding dub reggae influences alongside orchestral melodies and jungle bass weighted sounds. After releasing many 12-inch singles on Big Apple, they founded DMZ Records.

In 2005, dubstep continued to build momentum: The DMZ label gained strength, Rinse FM radio sets became available on online sharing sites, the www.dubstepforum was launched, and global online media outlets began to show interest in this genre (and the UK scene). At this same time, Digital Mystikz (along with Loefah and Sgt. Pokes) began to manage a bi-monthly South London party called DMZ. It was held at a 400-person location called 3rd Bass—the basement room of Mass, a converted Brixton church (once the site of many legendary jungle events). This scene percolated until 2006, during DMZ's first anniversary night gathering. An outdoor line of 600+ people forced the club to move the dubstep congregation from its smaller side room into the main (large) room. This was a visual and substantial landmark in UK's dubstep crossover popularity.

Suddenly (in 2006), bass heavy DJs were getting bookings, not only at FWD>> or DMZ, but also in Leeds and Bristol. In addition, Digital Mystikz and Loefah were DJing all over Europe, while Skream and Kode9 were playing New York, San Francisco, Tokyo, Los Angeles, or Barcelona. As if that were not enough, dubstep vinyl pressing sales shot up into the thousands, rather than the usual 200–300 copies. Increased record sales and growing audiences gave way to one huge musical impact as well. The scene's core producers (Kode9, Burial, Distance, Benga, and Skream) now gained the traction and confidence to tackle the long-play full-album format. (Dubstep artists usually produced 1–2 tracks on a 12-inch record per release.) By year's end, major motion pictures included dubstep tracks within their soundtracks, too.

In 2007, dubstep had reached deeply into other media streams. Benga, Skream, and other dubstep producers provided the soundtrack to the second series of *Dubplate Drama*, which aired on channel 4 (a local UK public access television station). By this time, dubstep's influence had reached the U.S. pop scene, too, most notably with Britney Spears' track "Freakshow." Critics immediately noticed the influence of dubstep sounds and "wobble" bass effects.

In late 2008, a limited 12-inch featuring Lee Scratch Perry and Prince Far-I was released under the pseudonym "Iron Devil." This was the first recorded example of a Jamaican dub founder acknowledging dubstep and creating new music within the genre. This solidified the connection between dubstep and its Jamaican dub heritage. Thus, it was now clear that dubstep had reached the masses in both the UK and USA. It captured the hearts of listeners, as well as the ears of mainstream media (and pop culture).

STEADY PROGRESS AND CROSSOVER

In 2010, dubstep songs like "I Need Air" by Magnetic Man started appearing on the UK pop charts. In 2010–2011, progressive artists such as Flux Pavilion, Noisia, Bassnectar, and Zeds Dead began to redefine the traditional dub sound by employing more mid-range bass frequencies (and a four-on-the-floor pulse) within their mixes. Not only did this build a bridge between progressive house and traditional UK bass, but it also formed a more high-powered mix style through the use of the (now immensely popular) "bass drop" (discussed in the characteristics chapter, page 26). In tandem, American producer Skrillex achieved commercial success with his dubstep-influenced EP *Scary Monsters and Nice Sprites*, which reached number three on the U.S. Billboard Dance and Electronic album charts.

Recently, dubstep's influence has also further permeated the U.S. commercial market. Britney Spears built on her 2007 dubstep hit "Freakshow" with a follow up, "Hold It Against Me." Almost immediately, UK artists like Rusko, Chase & Status, and Nero were producing (or remixing) tracks for major pop acts such as Rihanna, Cee-Lo Green, Katy Perry, and Lady Gaga. Once these tracks were on the airwaves, large outdoor festivals such as Bonnaroo, Coachella, Electric Daisy Carnival, and Burning Man booked dubstep DJs as main acts. Fueled by club culture (and these new events), Bassnectar and Skrillex aggressively toured rock halls that hadn't previously hosted DJs. Furthermore, newer festivals, like North Coast in Chicago, also began to tailor themselves to the urban audience and cross-section of jam, hip-hop, and dubstep. Urban acts like Snoop Dogg released his dub-esque record *Throw Your Dubs Up*, and Jay-Z and Kanye West employed dubs textures on "Who Gon Stop Me." It was clear: Dubstep now looked, sounded, and was successful like both hip-hop and rock and roll.

BROSTEP AND AMERICAN DEVELOPMENT

In 2011, dubstep gained a hefty footing in the U.S. market with the help of a September 2011 *Spin* magazine EDM (electronic dance music) special. It featured Skrillex and referred to brostep as a "lurching and aggressive" variant of dubstep that is commercially successful in U.S. markets. Unlike traditional dubstep production styles that emphasize ultra-low bass frequencies, brostep accentuates the middle register. Thus, the sub-sonic bass was gradually giving way to distorted bass riffs that functioned roughly within the same register as an electric guitar.

As if this were not enough, the popular heavy metal act Korn began to blend its mid-range frequency rock instrumentation with dubstep. With the help of many electronic producers such as Skrillex, Noisia, Excision, drum-and-bass innovators 12th Planet and Downlink and Feed Me, they released *Path of Totality*. This record sold 19 million units worldwide and further cemented the affiliation between electronic dubstep and the traditional sounds of heavy metal.

It's important to note that dubstep purists do not consider this American variation true dubstep. However, there is no denying that this style has permeated all genres of music.

TODAY

Traditionalists like Burial point to the sonic superiority of classic dubstep, with its dynamic analog bass lines and complex arrangement patterns that focus on heart-stopping sub bass. However, there is certainly room for artists like Grammy-award-winning Skrillex and Korn, who choose to focus on progressive bass lines, heavy digital distortion, and gut-wrenching synth drop sections that maintain the sub bass while covering more of the frequency spectrum. Whichever subcategory of dubstep you prefer, this music is becoming a mainstream form of dance music around the world.

Chapter 3: Characteristics of Dubstep

Coki (of Digital mystikz)

Okay, you've read the influences section and history overview, and listened to a couple of tracks online, but how can we define or identify a true debstep track? In broad terms, dubstep is dub (reggae) music set to a UK two-step (half-time) beat. It's important to note that this genre does not rely on the typical electronic four-to-the-floor beat, but rather spaced, syncopated hi-hats and percussion. Samples are then laid over low-frequency (typically oscillating) bass lines, which give the listener an immense sense of movement and insistence. Song forms are then created with the use of introductions, bass drops, riffs, and intro reprises and outros. Thereafter, rewinds and hard leads are added for dramatic effect. However (and in recent pop music), these hard leads and rewinds have been replaced with vocal hooks, verses, and choruses. Let's take a look at these various characteristics (and components) of a typical dubstep composition in detail.

GROOVE: BREAKING DOWN THE COMPONENTS

Dubstep rhythms range between 138–150 beats per minute, are syncopated, and oftentimes make great use of glitch-esque stuttering patterns. In its early stages, dubstep was often more percussive, with more influences from 2-step drum patterns. Let's take a look at a basic 2-step beat.

2-step beat

A typical 2-step drum pattern features a kick on the first and third beat, with syncopated rhythms applied to other elements of the percussion, such as the hi-hat, snare drum, woodblocks, and tambourine. These can be phrased as either straight or swung. In addition, tracks with half-note kicks are also perceived as being slower than the traditional four-on-the-floor beat used within house and techno. This eighth-note example is the basis for all 2-step patterns:

In addition, placing the kick drum on the "and" of beat three is the most common variation. Like this:

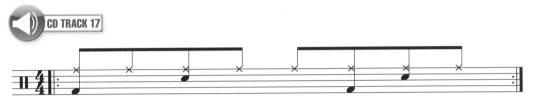

Finally, accents can be added to every upbeat on the hi-hat:

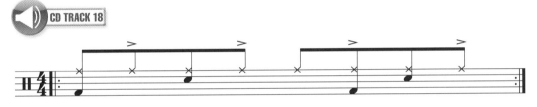

Of course, there are thousands of 2-step groove variations. As such, the examples above merely serve as an overview, or "entrance," into the world of the basic 2-step.

dubstep beat

Unlike the 2-step that emphasizes both beats one and three on the kick, a dubstep pattern only emphasizes the one. Not only does this give the impression of an even slower tempo (than a 2-step), but it is also paired with a snare or clap on beat three to form a half-time groove. The remaining percussive elements (hi-hat, shakers, etc.) remain in a normal meter, which then feels like a double-time phrase. This eighth-note example is the basis for all dubstep patterns:

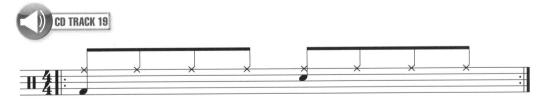

Drumkit-wise (both programmed and acoustic), many devices are employed to the basic half-time pattern, which helps to create forward momentum. Let's take a look at four of the main tactics employed:

1. To create a syncopated thump, sixteenth-note kick drum patterns can be added:

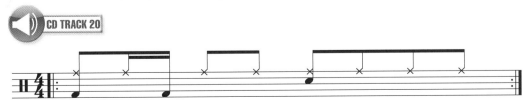

2. This can be augmented with accents that are placed on the hi-hat. These can be
   a. Used alone (with the original half-time pattern):

   b. Used with a sixteenth-note kick drum pattern. As an example, I've placed these accents within No. 1's kick drum phrase like this:

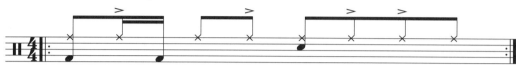

3. Sixteenth notes can also be utilized (with or without accents). As an example, this technique has been combined with both No. 1's kick drum pattern and No. 2's hi-hat accents:

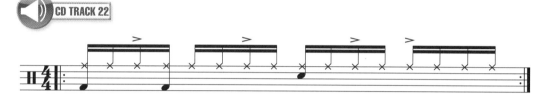

4. Oftentimes (and for a complete rhythmic departure), quarter-note triplets are employed, either:
   a. Within a half-time pattern (i.e., kick on beat one and snare on beat three):

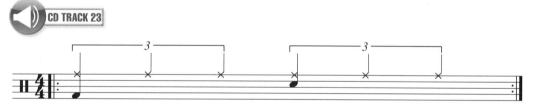

   b. Or with additional kick drums placed within the rhythmic structure:

Altogether, these can be combined into one cumulative groove like this:

wobble-bass

The most common harmonic characteristic of dubstep is its "wobble-bass" bass line. This extended bass note is manipulated digitally with a low-frequency oscillator that controls additional parameters of a synthesizer, which include volume, distortion, and other filter permutations. These permutations are then altered—played as a combination of quarter, eighth, sixteenth, or thirty-second note straight and triplet rhythms. Producers can also employ these same synthesizer settings within software programs to achieve this oscillating effect. Whichever tool a producer uses, these effects are usually synched to the tempo of the song. Here is an example of a software synthesizer's LFO (and related) controls:

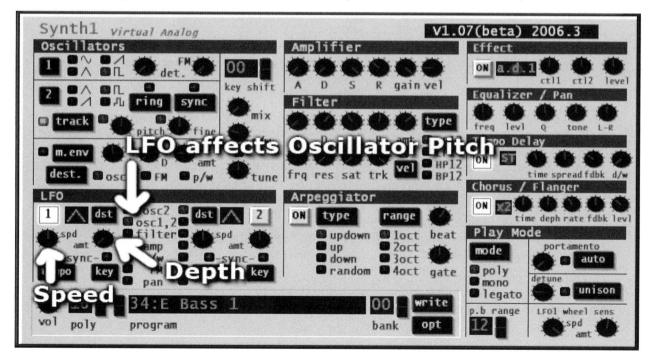

The LFO controls the speed of the filter's rhythmic variation, which in turn, creates the wobble. Occasionally, these wobble tones reach as low as 20 hertz (the lowest frequency that humans can hear). In addition, these textures require special speaker systems to convey the rumbling sound properly, which is one large reason that this style is so club-friendly. When you hear people discuss dubstep's "wub wub wub" sound, they are referring to the wobble-bass that is used within the majority of today's dubstep tracks.

LFO and Filter Rhythmic Example: Here is an example of an extended bass note that is altered with various filters. This extended tone cycles through the following rhythmic values as follows:

ADDITIONAL ATTRIBUTES: SONG STRUCTURE

Dubstep is usually comprised of the following sections:

- **An intro:** This section establishes the sonic textures and motif. These items usually include (but are not limited to) a sparse (or incrementally built) drum groove, arpeggiated synth pattern (or textural pad), and in recent years, a vocal breakdown.

- **The bass drop:** This is what made dubstep popular, and it is where the wobble-bass is most prevalent. Typically, the drum groove will drop out or the existing intro track will start to fade into the background. After a brief pause, the overwhelming bass drop invades the track and it continues throughout the rest of the section. This drop is also placed alongside a sonically heavier drum groove.

- **The riff:** This section (a repeating modulated bass riff) usually follows the drop. Whereas most bass drops will include at least three different musical notes at some point, this section relies on repeating the same motif as the intro alongside new elements. Rather than the bass drop's "wub wub" sound, the bass riff will sound like "yob yob."

- **An Outro:** A repetitive vamp where the tune either fades out or comes to a crashing endpoint. Rhythmically, many artists also return to a normal two-and-four backbeat, which implies a double-time feel over the original half-time melodies and motifs.

Example: I have listed one popular dubstep song form below:

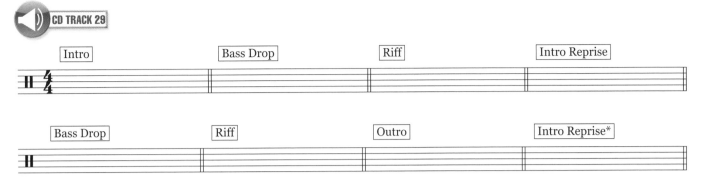

*A reprise is the repetition or reiteration of the opening material later in a composition.

In recent years, dubstep tracks have borrowed heavily from popular devices, including vocal verses and choruses. Oftentimes (when these items are used), the bass drop and main riff will be substituted with either a full vocal chorus or vocal breakdown. The breakdown is placed alongside percussive breaks, and no formal drumkit-esque pattern is present. Other times, they merely coexist with the more traditional elements of a dubstep track.

THE REWIND (AKA RELOAD)

This standard technique is utilized within most UK pirate radio garage, jungle, and dubstep nights. If a song seems to be especially popular on the dance floor, the DJ will "spin back" or *rewind* the record by hand without lifting the stylus, in order to play the track again.

Using the previous song form as an example, I have augmented the last intro reprise with a rewind (reload). Not only does this help to transition back into the first bass drop, but by starting the track over again, it also keeps people on the dance floor. For example:

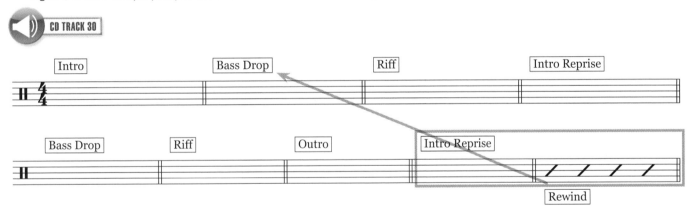

THE HARD LEAD

This sound usually plays the main solo and melodic elements within the intro and riff sections. Although it sounds like a new sound, the lead is usually a synth bass sound pitched up two to three octaves.

ALL TOGETHER

Using all the elements discussed, I have employed a basic dubstep chart for your review. Please note that a D.S. al Coda is used to repeat both the bass drop and riff, which then leads into the last intro reprise and outro.

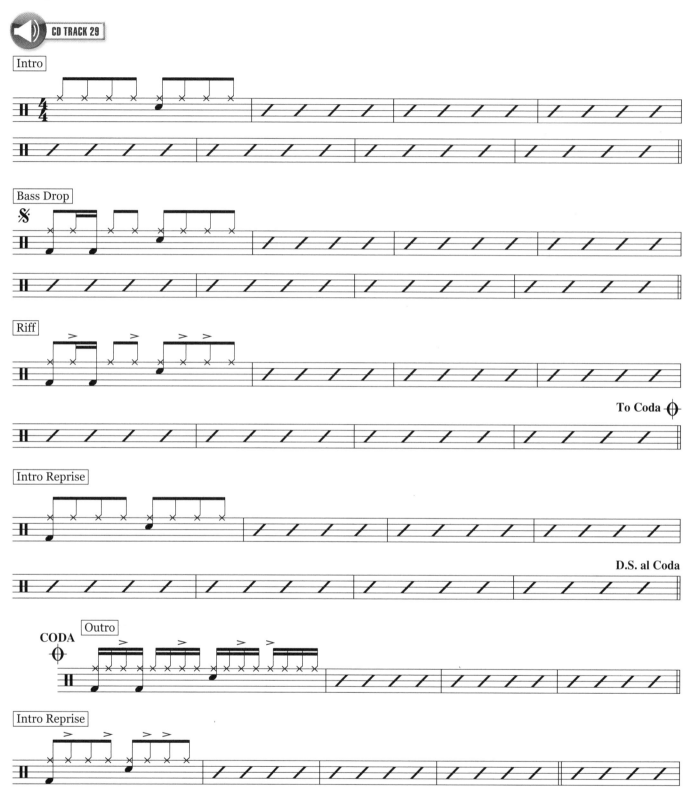

TIME TO GROOVE!

Now that we have discussed the various elements within dubstep, it is time to build your dub-savvy groove vocabulary and drumkit practice strategy. So let's begin with the preliminary quarter and eighth-note half-time development exercises.

Chapter 4: Quarter and Eighth-Note Half-Time Grooves

Practice Media	Tempos
Syncopated Percussion	90, 100, 110, 120, 130, 142 bpm
Synthesizer Loops	110, 125, 137, 142 bpm
Performance Loops	125, 137, 142, 150 bpm

QUARTER-NOTE HI-HAT GROOVES

In order to get acquainted with dubstep and its grooves, I have listed many preliminary quarter-note hi-hat half-time grooves for your review. Not only will these help you to phrase your snare on beat three, but they will also serve as the basis for the remaining chapters. Let's take a look at each exercise in great detail.

MAIN QUARTER-NOTE PHRASE

Our main hand pattern is comprised of a quarter-note hi-hat pattern and single snare drum on beat three:

CD TRACK 33

In order to develop the musical "know-how" and independence to play quarter-note hi-hat half-time patterns, you must first work through all three sections. These include: (1) the kick drum on beats one and two, (2) the kick drum on beats three and four, and (3) the kick drum combination exercises.

1. kick drum on beats one and two

These exercises isolate the eighth notes that precede beat three on the snare drum:

2. kick drum on beats three and four

These exercises isolate the eighth notes that follow beat three on the snare drum:

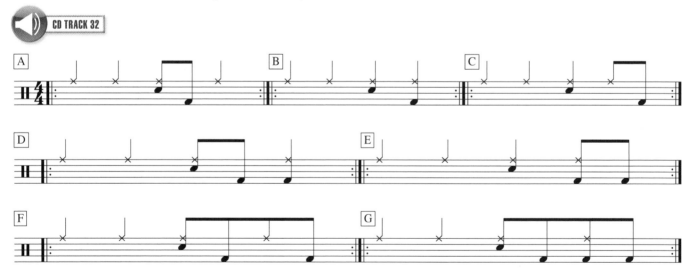

3. kick drum combinations

Now that you are comfortable with placing your kick drum on each isolated beat, let's combine the previous exercises into denser phrases. As an example, I've employed the kick patterns from both No. 1 (kick drum on beats one and two) and letter A (kick drum on beats three and four). Once these are laid atop one another, they form the first combination exercise 1A. For example:

This method is used to create each (and every) mathematical permutation of exercises 1–8 and A–G. Let's begin with 1A–1G:

1A–1G

The following exercises utilize exercise No. 1 and A–G:

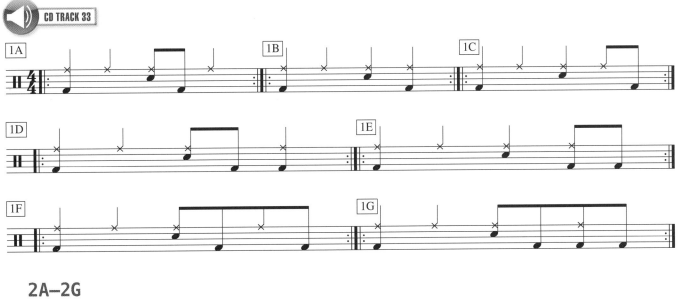

2A–2G

The following exercises utilize exercise No. 2 and A–G:

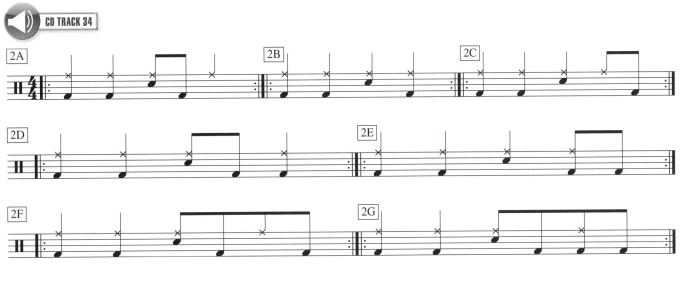

3A–3G

The following exercises utilize exercise No. 3 and A–G:

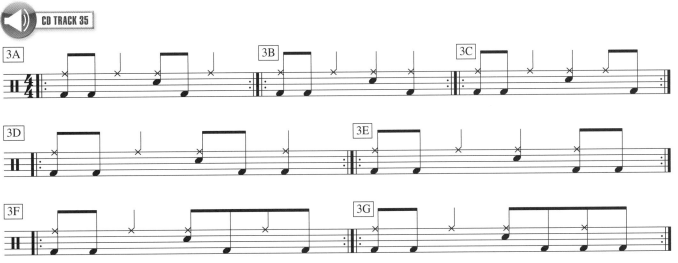

quarter and eighth-note half-time grooves   31

4A–4G

The following exercises utilize exercise No. 4 and A–G:

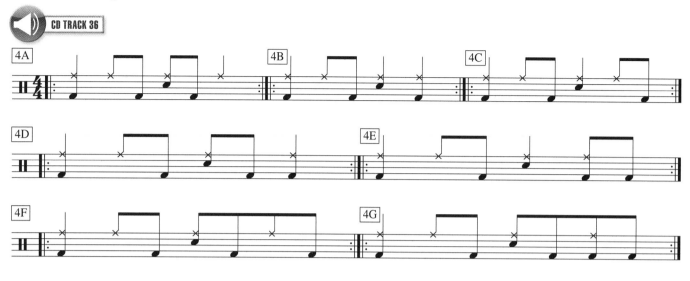

5A–5G

The following exercises utilize exercise No. 5 and A–G:

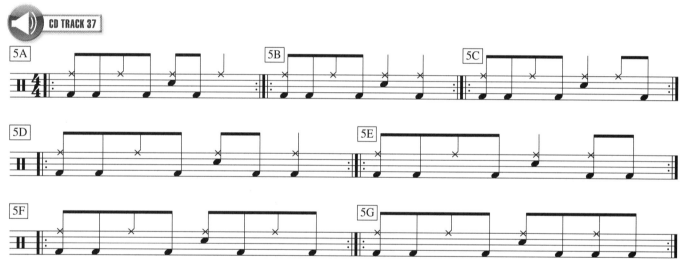

6A–6G

The following exercises utilize exercise No. 6 and A–G:

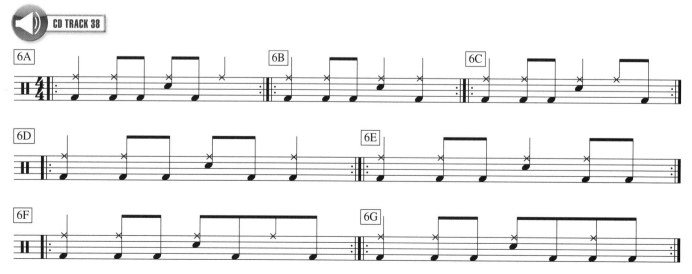

7A–7G

The following exercises utilize exercise No. 7 and A–G:

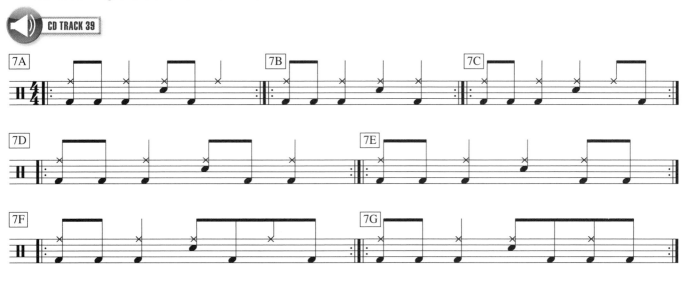

8A–8G

The following exercises utilize exercise No. 8 and A–G:

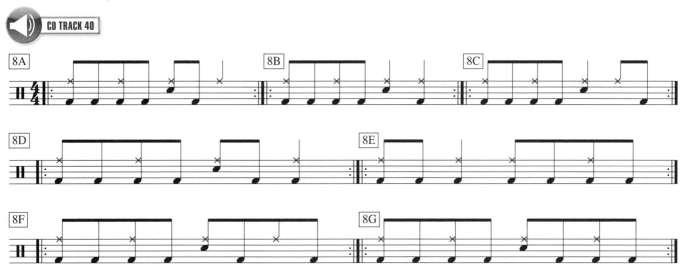

BACKING MATERIAL: APPLYING WHAT YOU HAVE LEARNED

Now that you have combined many of the previous quarter-note hi-hat phrases alongside both quarter and eighth-note kick drum patterns, let's apply them to music. I have omitted notated drum grooves below. Therefore, feel free to improvise with your favorite kick drum patterns and apply what you have been practicing!

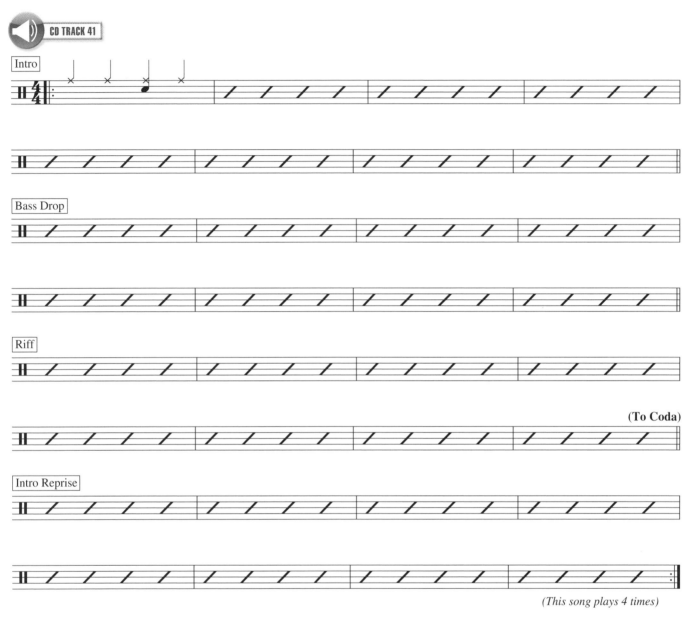

(This song plays 4 times)

MAIN EIGHTH–NOTE PHRASE

Our main hand pattern is comprised of an eighth-note hi-hat pattern and single snare drum on beat three:

In order to develop the musical "know-how" and independence to play half-time patterns, you must first work through all three eighth-note sections. These include: (1) the kick drum on beats one and two, (2) the kick drum on beats three and four, and (3) the kick drum combination exercises.

1. placing the kick drum on beats one and two

These exercises isolate the eighth notes that precede beat three on the snare drum:

2. placing the kick drum on beats three and four

These exercises isolate the eighth notes that follow beat three on the snare drum:

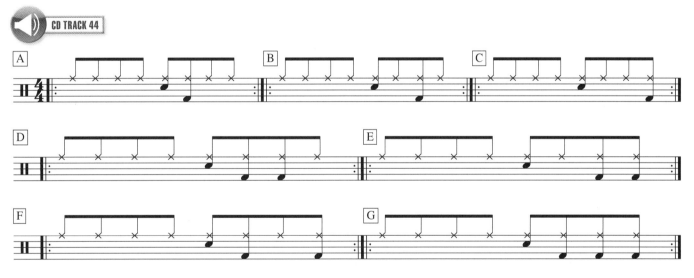

3. kick drum combinations

Now that you are comfortable with placing your kick drum on each isolated beat, let's combine the previous exercises into denser phrases. As an example, I've employed the kick patterns from both No. 1 (kick drum on beats one and two) and letter A (kick drum placed on beats three and four). Once these are laid atop one another, they form the first combination exercise 1A. For example:

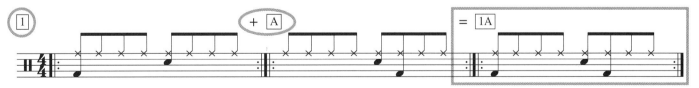

This method is used to create each (and every) mathematical permutation of exercises 1–8 and A–G. Let's begin with 1A–1G:

1A–1G

The following exercises utilize exercise No. 1 and A–G:

2A–2G

The following exercises utilize exercise No. 2 and A–G:

3A–3G

The following exercises utilize exercise No. 3 and A–G:

4A–4G

The following exercises utilize exercise No. 4 and A–G:

CD TRACK 48

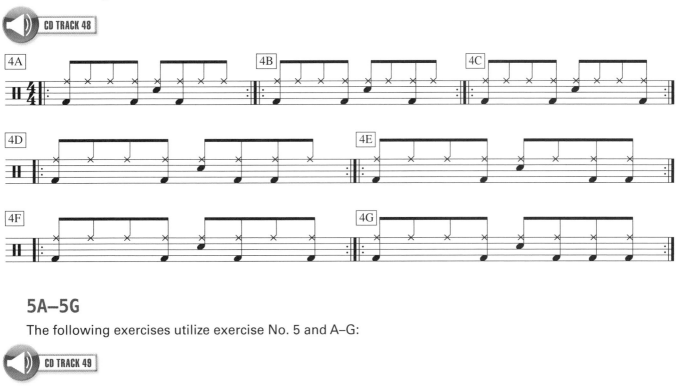

5A–5G

The following exercises utilize exercise No. 5 and A–G:

CD TRACK 49

6A–6G

The following exercises utilize exercise No. 6 and A–G:

CD TRACK 50

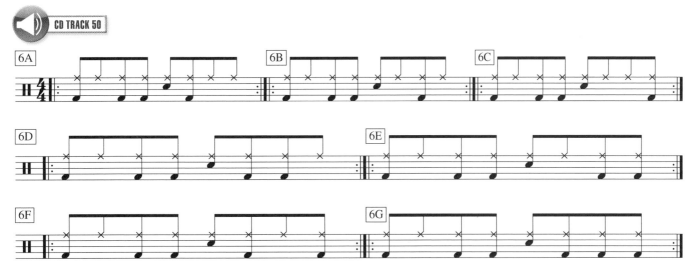

7A–7G

The following exercises utilize exercise No. 7 and A–G:

8A–8G

The following exercises utilize exercise No. 8 and A–G:

ADDITIONAL PRACTICE METHOD: TWO-HANDED SIXTEENTH-NOTE HI-HAT

Now that you have practiced (and mastered) the individual eighth-note exercises for each beat (and combination thereof), I have listed two bonus one-measure hand ostinatos for further practice.

A two-handed sixteenth-note pattern is employed in this first ostinato. You'll notice that the right hand plays the snare alone on beat three (i.e., no hi-hat) as follows:

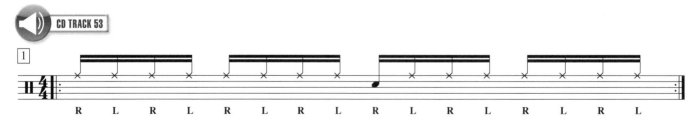

Finally, accents are added to beats two and four on the hi-hat like this:

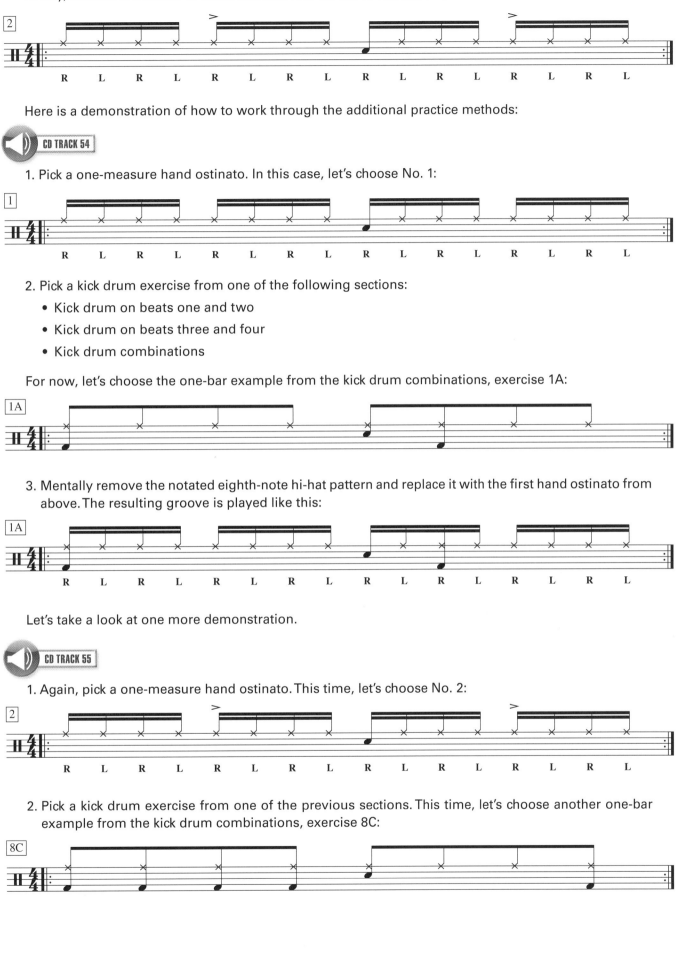

Here is a demonstration of how to work through the additional practice methods:

CD TRACK 54

1. Pick a one-measure hand ostinato. In this case, let's choose No. 1:

2. Pick a kick drum exercise from one of the following sections:
   - Kick drum on beats one and two
   - Kick drum on beats three and four
   - Kick drum combinations

For now, let's choose the one-bar example from the kick drum combinations, exercise 1A:

3. Mentally remove the notated eighth-note hi-hat pattern and replace it with the first hand ostinato from above. The resulting groove is played like this:

Let's take a look at one more demonstration.

CD TRACK 55

1. Again, pick a one-measure hand ostinato. This time, let's choose No. 2:

2. Pick a kick drum exercise from one of the previous sections. This time, let's choose another one-bar example from the kick drum combinations, exercise 8C:

3. Mentally remove the notated eighth-note hi-hat pattern and replace it with the second hand ostinato from the previous page. The resulting groove is played like this:

BACKING MATERIAL: APPLYING WHAT YOU HAVE LEARNED

Now that you have combined many of the previous kick drum phrases alongside the two hand ostinatos, let's apply them to music. You'll notice that I have placed one ostinato within the intro and bass drop, and the remaining one within the riff and intro reprise sections. As the kick drum pattern is omitted, feel free to improvise with your favorite kick drum patterns below:

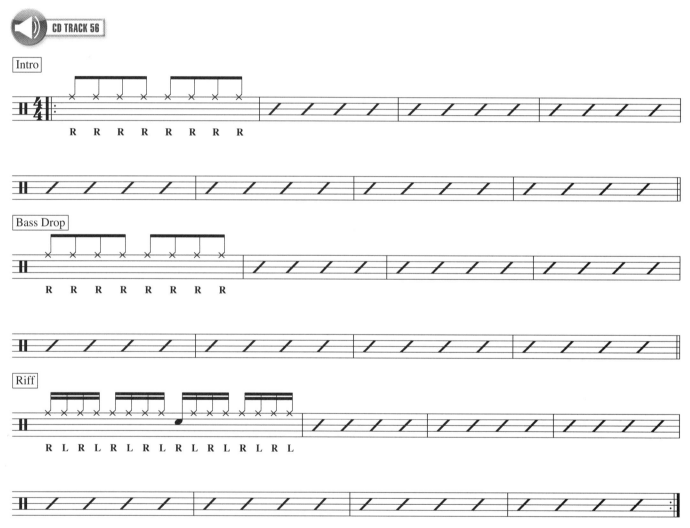

(This song plays 4 times)

Chapter 5: Offbeat Eighth and Sixteenth Half-Time Grooves

Practice Media	Tempos
Syncopated Percussion	90, 110, 130, 142 bpm
Synthesizer Loops	125, 137, 142 bpm
Performance Loops	125, 137, 142, 150 bpm

Now that you have become comfortable with the previous quarter and eighth-note sections, let's expand your half-time rhythmic horizons and move on to offbeat eighth and syncopated sixteenth-note kick drum patterns. It's important to realize that many of these kick rhythms do not line up with the hi-hat or play on beat one. Thus (and if you have never done this before), it can be quite challenging, especially between 120–150 bpm!

OFFBEAT EIGHTH– AND SIXTEENTH–NOTE KICK DRUM FRAGMENTS

The following one-beat fragments isolate (and are placed on) beats one, two, three, and four. For the sake of brevity (and for our future groove-creation methods), the hi-hat has been intentionally omitted.

kick drum fragments : beat one

These grooves continue the numbering format from Chapter 4 and isolate the kick drum notes on beat one. (For the sake of continuity, you'll notice that numbers 9 and 11 are identical to numbers 1 and 3 from the previous chapter. This is intentional and helps to keep the sixteenth flow and connection between exercises.)

kick drum fragments : beat two

kick drum fragments: beat three

In addition to isolating the sixteenth-note kick drum phrases on beat three, the following exercises continue the lettering convention from exercises A–G in the previous chapter.

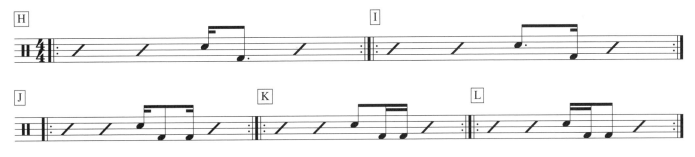

kick drum fragments: beat four

In addition to isolating the sixteenth-note kick drum phrases on beat four, the following exercises continue the lettering convention from the previous exercises (H–L).

USING THE FRAGMENTS: OUR TWO MAIN PATTERNS

You should work through the following fragments alongside our two main half-time hand patterns.

Here's a brief demonstration on how to utilize these fragments:

🔊 CD TRACK 57

Beat one: If you were working through number 10 alongside the quarter-note hi-hat phrase, it would be played as follows:

However, if you were using the eighth-note hi-hat, it would be played like this:

Beat two: If you picked number 22 and utilized the quarter-note hi-hat, it would sound like this:

Again, employing the eighth-note hi-hat phrase with example 22, it would be played as follows:

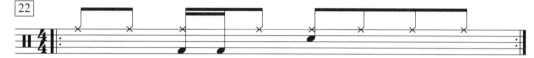

Beat three: Should you choose to work through fragment H (alongside the quarter-note hi-hat pattern), it would be played like this:

Here's fragment H alongside the eighth-note hi-hat pattern:

Beat four: Finally, placing letter T within both hand patterns sounds like this:

The quarter-note hi-hat pattern:

The eighth-note hi-hat pattern:

ADDITIONAL PRACTICE METHOD:
TWO-HANDED SIXTEENTH-NOTE HI-HAT

Now that you have practiced (and mastered) the individual sixteenth-note fragments for each beat, I have re-enlisted our two one-measure hand ostinatos (and a new third) in the following examples.

To review, a two-handed sixteenth-note pattern is employed within the first ostinato. You'll notice that the right hand plays the snare alone on beat three (i.e., no hi-hat) as follows:

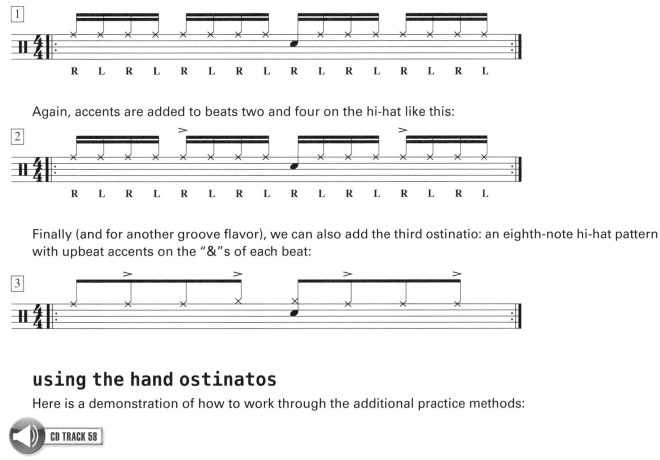

R L R L R L R L R L R L R L R L

Again, accents are added to beats two and four on the hi-hat like this:

R L R L R L R L R L R L R L R L

Finally (and for another groove flavor), we can also add the third ostinatio: an eighth-note hi-hat pattern with upbeat accents on the "&"s of each beat:

using the hand ostinatos

Here is a demonstration of how to work through the additional practice methods:

CD TRACK 58

1. Pick a one-measure hand ostinato. In this case, let's choose No. 2:

R L R L R L R L R L R L R L R L

2. Pick a kick drum exercise from one of the following fragment sections, placing the kick drum on beat one, two, three, or four.

For now, let's choose fragment 12 (from the kick on beat one section):

3. Overlay the second hand ostinato from above. The resulting groove is played like this:

R L R L R L R L R L R L R L R L

However, if you were to use the third upbeat eighth ostinato, it would be played like this:

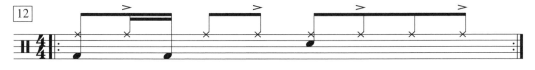

BUILDING SIXTEENTH-NOTE KICK DRUM GROOVE COMBINATIONS

Obviously, the last few pages of patterns isolate each beat and are quite static in their approach. So how can you create interesting (and grooving) sixteenth kick-based dubstep patterns with the fragments on the previous pages? Well, let's use fragments 9–32 (beats one and two) within fragments H–T (beats three and four).

Here is a demonstration on how to make your own combination exercises:

option 1: beats one and two combined

- Pick one fragment from numbers 9–20 (placing the kick drum on beat one).
- Pick one fragment from numbers 21–32 (placing the kick drum on beat two).
- Choose a hi-hat pattern (quarter notes, eighth notes, or any of the ostinatos).

Thus, if you picked fragments 14 and 29 and combined them within the quarter-note hi-hat pattern, it would be played as follows:

option 2: beats one and three combined

- Pick one fragment from numbers 9–20 (placing the kick drum on beat one).
- Pick one fragment from letters H–L (placing the kick drum on beat three).
- Choose a hi-hat pattern (quarter notes, eighth notes, or any of the ostinatos).
- Thus, if you picked fragments 14 and letter I and combined them within the eighth-note hi-hat pattern, it would be played as follows:

option 3: beats one and four combined

- Pick one fragment from numbers 9–20 (placing the kick drum on beat one).
- Pick one fragment from letters M–T (placing the kick drum on beat four).
- Choose a hi-hat pattern (quarter notes, eighth notes or any of the ostinatos).

Thus, if you picked fragments 14 and letter T and combined them within the quarter note hi-hat pattern, it would be played as follows:

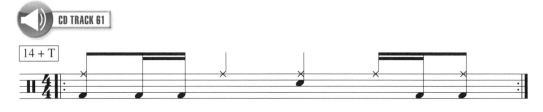

option 4: adding a sixteenth-note hi-hat pattern to options 1–3

If you added a two-handed sixteenth-note pattern to 14+T above, it would sound like this:

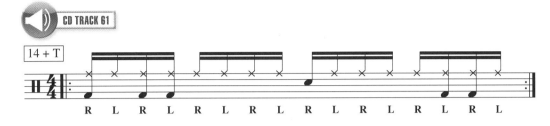

ADDITIONAL PRACTICE METHOD: VOICING ON THE SNARE DRUM

In addition to playing eighth and sixteenth fragments on the kick drum, select dubstep grooves apply these same syncopated rhythms to the snare drum. These are usually placed on beat three, and I've listed the most commonly used ideas below. (In order to differentiate this section from the kick drum fragments, I have labeled these exercises with lower-case letters.)

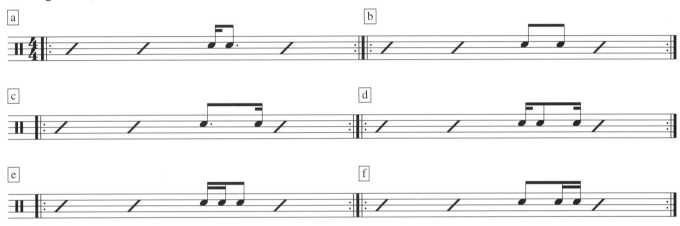

Here is a brief demonstration on how you can apply these fragments to your kit:

If you chose letter f while working through number 10 alongside the quarter-note hi-hat phrase, it would be played as follows:

However, if you were using the eighth-note hi-hat, it would be played like this:

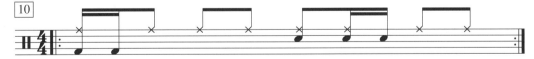

Obviously, the number of variations and grooves that we can create using the one-beat kick and snare drum fragment charts is limitless. Thus, this method is meant to serve as an entrance point into the world of sixteenth kick combinations and unlock your own creativity.

BACKING MATERIAL : APPLYING WHAT YOU HAVE LEARNED

Now that you have combined (and mastered) many of the previous sixteenth kick drum fragments, it's time to apply them to music. With this in mind, I have placed one sixteenth fragment with each section below. These are placed on beat one, which will allow you to improvise your kick drum on the remaining beats alongside each hi-hat pattern (quarter notes, eighth notes, or any of the ostinatos).

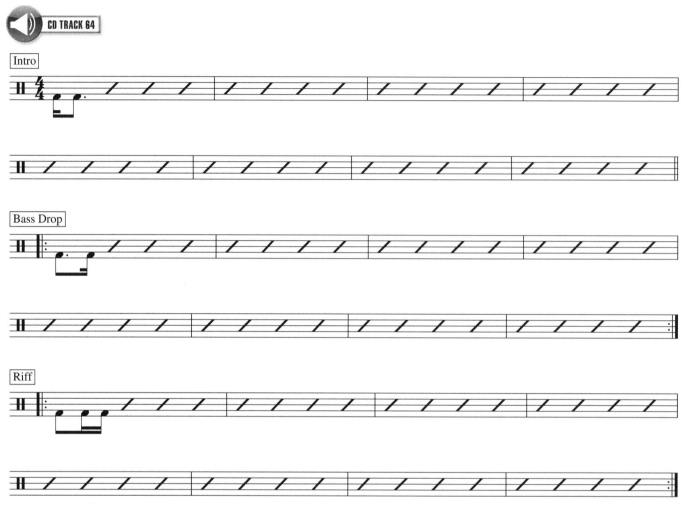

(This song plays 4 times)

Chapter 6: Adding Sixteenth-Note Hi-Hat Patterns

Mary Ann Hobbs

SYNCOPATED HI–HATS

Listen to any Dubstep track. What makes the song groove and flow as you are listening to it? Does is feel like a train that cannot be stopped? Is the rhythm so incessant and repetitive that it could groove for days without wavering in its consistency? Are you tapping your foot without even realizing it? If you answered "yes" to any of these questions, then you also realize the exact reason why many dub artists program syncopated hi-hat patterns alongside a static half-time drum groove: They add a relentless, repetitive, and unwavering forward momentum to a conventional kick and snare pattern. As a result, you must master a few genre-specific sixteenth-note hi-hat partials, which will add momentum and an inherent drive to your grooves.

Remember, *you are not a drum machine*—but you must give the listener the impression that you are! So in order to maintain that illusion, you must think like a programmer, DJ, and producer who modifies their half-time phrases with syncopated sixteenth-note hi-hat partials. This not only helps keep the music flowing, but it also makes the drum part sound as if it were programmed.

So, how can you think like a DJ and keep the momentum going, in addition to playing a stylistically correct hi-hat pattern?

Thought 1

What item is lacking in nearly every programmed groove? Answer: dynamics! So when you are playing a hi-hat pattern (and full groove), it should be devoid of any traditional drumset dynamics. The kick, snare, and hi-hat should have roughly the same volume, as if they were typed into Ableton Live's piano roll.

Thought 2

Note choice is important, too. Dubstep grooves are built not only by syncopated hi-hat patterns, but also by adding additional sounds (and subtle variations) within those patterns. These grooves can feature multiple hi-hat sounds, white noise, and even tambourine within the original syncopated pattern!

Thought 3

Two-handed stickings are needed to navigate many of these phrases. These rhythms are executed by the left hand reaching over within a static eighth-note hi-hat pattern. Not only are dubstep grooves usually 130 bpm and above, but this method also ensures that your groove does not waver in its consistency.

GROOVE CREATION 1:
PRELIMINARY SYNCOPATED HI–HAT EXERCISES

So how do I create interesting and grooving dubstep hi-hat patterns? Well, I utilize the following one-beat hi-hat fragments (sixteenth-note partials) within a standard eighth-note groove. This way, I am able to serve the music, complement the wobble-bass lines, and make the club goers dance to my forward momentum. Let's take a look at these one-beat fragments:

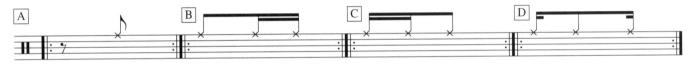

Now that we have reviewed the one-beat fragments and established that the hi-hat voice adds forward momentum to a half-time groove, let's begin to combine these fragments into their own distinctive 4/4 groove patterns. I have outlined a few simple steps for building our new and interesting dubstep beats below.

hi–hat placement key

hi–hat placement chart

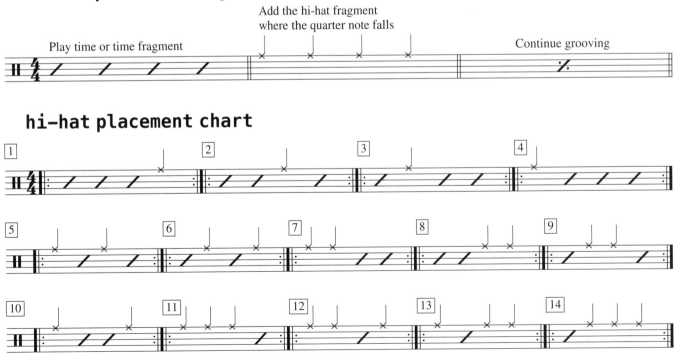

Here is a demonstration of how to work through the one-measure hi-hat fragment exercises:

1. Pick a one-beat hi-hat fragment. In this case, let's choose hi-hat fragment letter A.

2. Pick a one-measure hi-hat placement. In this case, let's choose hi-hat placement No. 1.

3. Pick a groove from the previous chapters to perform with. This time, let's use exercise 3 (within the eighth-note chapter, page 35).

4. Now play the groove during the time slashes (in No. 2) and place the hi-hat fragment within the quarter-note hi-hat.

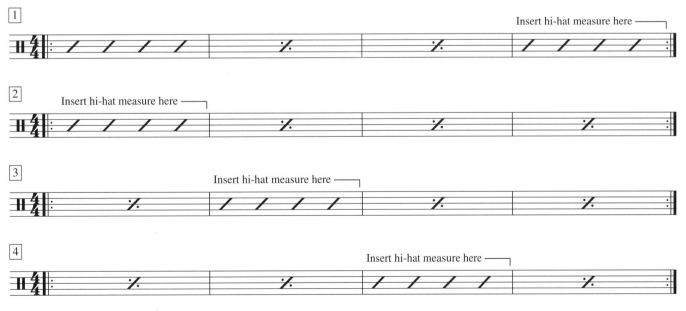

Once you have mastered any one of the hi-hat placement exercises, pick any media within the previous chapters and practice any placement exercise (Nos. 1–14) with one of the following hi-hat practice methods.

HI-HAT PRACTICE METHODS

Here is a demonstration of how to work through the previously mentioned hi-hat practice methods (along with one hi-hat fragment exercise):

1. Pick a hi-hat fragment. In this case, let's choose letter A once more.

2. Pick a one-measure hi-hat placement. Again, let's choose hi-hat placement No. 1.

3. Choose a groove example to perform with. For the sake of familiarity, let's choose exercise 3 (within the eighth-note chapter, page 35).

4. Next, pick one of the four hi-hat practice methods. In this case let's choose number one:

5. Finally, play three bars of time and on the fourth bar execute the hi-hat placement exercise.

Repeat this process for whichever hi-hat fragment exercise, placement, and practice method you choose.

ADDITIONAL SOUND SOURCES

In addition to the previously mentioned relentless hi-hat fragments, artists also use many hi-hat sounds to achieve interesting performance and sonic functions that an acoustic drummer cannot (on a single hi-hat).

For instance, how many times have you heard a dubstep hi-hat pattern that alternates between two (or three) hi-hat sounds? How about a super dry hi-hat that sounds so choked it could actually be a tabletop sample? Furthermore, you can probably even turn on your favorite Internet radio station and listen to programmed dubstep grooves that have flurries of hi-hat sixteenth-note figures that also incorporate a tambourine within its rhythms. These types of programming methods have textural and inhuman performance qualities that acoustic drummers do not immediately believe they can achieve on an acoustic hi-hat. Therefore, let's discuss how to replicate these ideas on an acoustic kit.

setup: two auxiliary hi-hats

In order to get the most out of this section, I suggest adding two auxiliary hi-hats to your acoustic drum setup. One set should be placed to the left of your main hi-hat and the other to the right, like this:

If you do not have three sets of hi-hats, do not worry! Two sets of splashes or crashes work well, too.

Application

Main Hi-Hat   Left Auxiliary Hi-Hat   Right Auxiliary Hi-Hat

Let's use the following three applications of this setup:

1. **Move your left hand:** For the sake of this demonstration, I have notated one of my favorite hi-hat fragment combinations (on beats three and four) here:

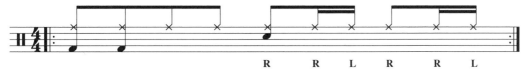

While performing on your main hi-hat, move all left-hand sixteenth-note fragment partials to the left auxiliary hi-hat like this:

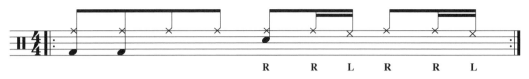

R   R   L   R   R   L

2. **Move your right hand:** While performing on your main hi-hat, move all right-hand sixteenth-note fragment partials to the right auxiliary hi-hat. (Note: your left hand should remain on the main hi-hat.) For example:

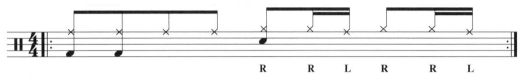

R   R   L   R   R   L

3. **Move both hands:** While performing on your main hi-hat, move both hands during the entire fragment. As such, all right-hand partials will move to the right auxiliary hi-hat and the left-hand partials to the left auxiliary hi-hat like this:

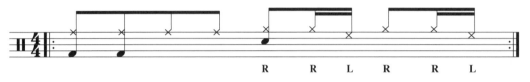

R   R   L   R   R   L

BACKING MATERIAL: APPLYING WHAT YOU HAVE LEARNED

Now that you have worked through many of the previous hi-hat phrases, let's apply them to music. As the drum notation is omitted, feel free to improvise with your favorite grooves and hi-hat patterns below:

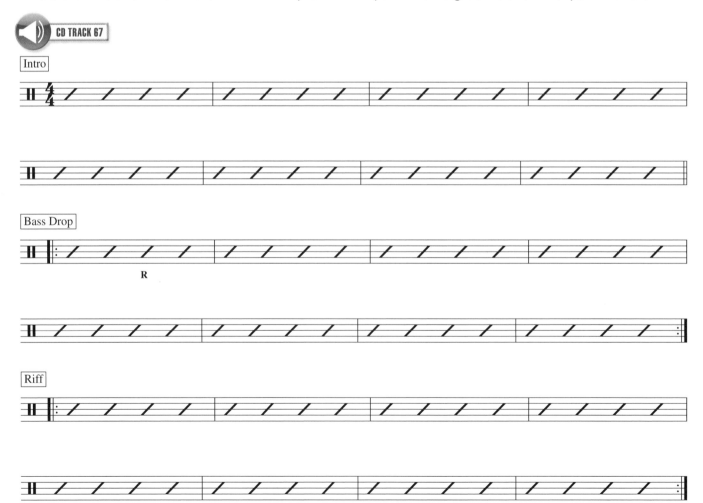

(This song plays 4 times)

Chapter 7: Quarter-Note Triplet Half-Time Grooves

Practice Media	Tempos
Syncopated Percussion	90, 110, 130, 142 bpm
Synthesizer Loops	125, 137, 142 bpm
Performance Loops	125, 137, 142, 150 bpm

Up to this point, we have concentrated exclusively on eighth- and sixteenth-note rhythms. However, many (if not most) dubstep producers also utilize quarter-note triplets. With this in mind, this chapter will help you to internalize these rhythms and gain the technique needed to perform these genre-specific grooves.

QUARTER-NOTE TRIPLET KICK DRUM FRAGMENTS

The following exercises place the kick drum within a full measure of quarter-note triplets:

BROKEN KICK DRUM FRAGMENTS

In order to mimic today's dubstep programming methods, the hi-hat no longer is played in unison with the kick drum.

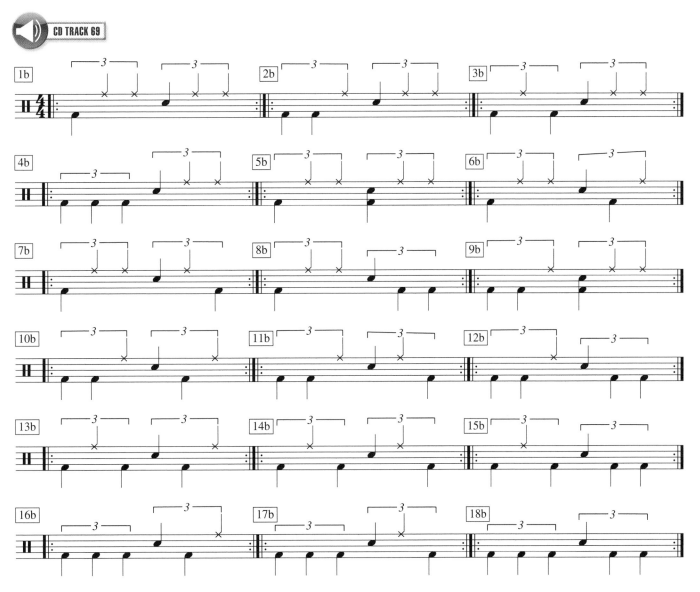

QUARTER–NOTE TRIPLET SNARE DRUM FRAGMENTS

The following exercises place the snare drum within a full measure of quarter-note triplets.

Notation reminder: A ghost note is a very quiet note that is felt rather than heard. It is notated like this:

Snare
Ghost
Note

BROKEN SNARE DRUM FRAGMENTS

In order to mimic today's dubstep programming methods, the hi-hat is not played in unison with the kick or snare drum.

CD TRACK 70

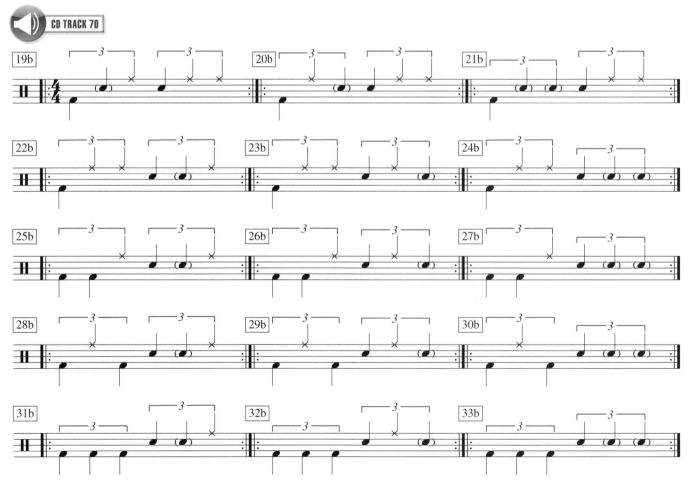

MIXED RHYTHMS

Many dubstep tracks combine straight and triplet rhythms. Not only are these rhythmically interesting, but also they lend a slight "jittery" feel to a track. Thus, I have listed many examples for your practice below.

Notation addition: Triplet fragment.

quarter-note triplets on beats one and two

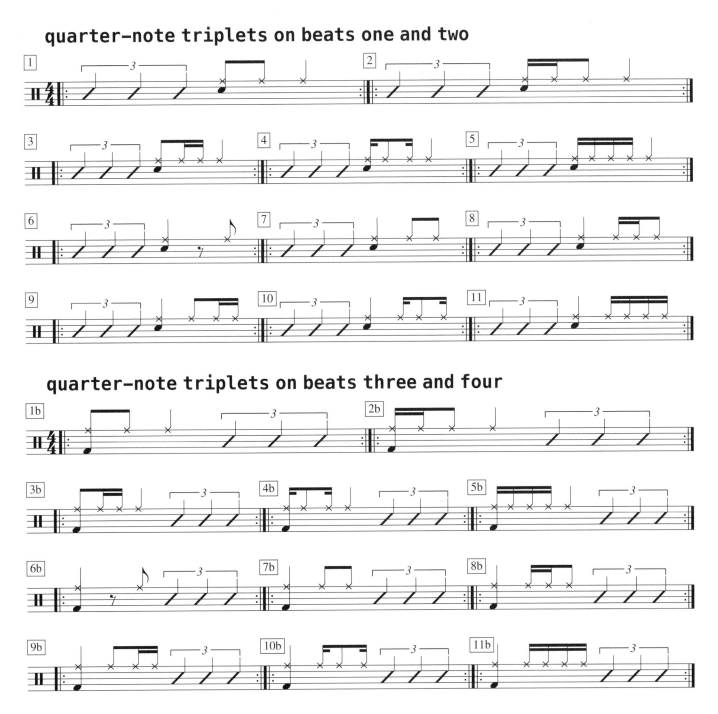

quarter-note triplets on beats three and four

Here is a demonstration of how to work through the mixed rhythm exercises within the "Quarter-Note Triplets on Beats One and Two" section.

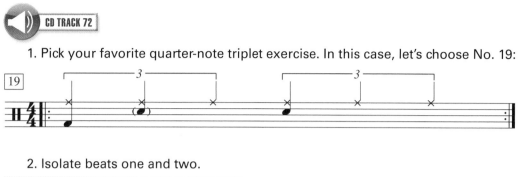

1. Pick your favorite quarter-note triplet exercise. In this case, let's choose No. 19:

2. Isolate beats one and two.

3. Choose a mixed rhythm exercise. For the sake of demonstration, let's employ No. 1.

4. Finally, place this two-beat isolation (from step No. 2 above) into the exercise. Thus, it would be played like this:

Here is a demonstration of how to work through the mixed rhythm exercises within the "Quarter-Note Triplets on Beats Three and Four" section:

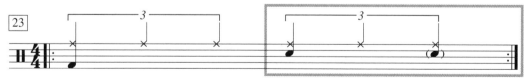

1. Pick your favorite quarter-note triplet exercise. In this case, let's choose No. 23.

2. Isolate beats three and four.

3. Choose a mixed rhythm exercise. For the sake of demonstration, let's employ No. 11b.

4. Finally, place this two-beat isolation (from step No. 2 above) into the exercise. Thus, it would be played like this:

mixed rhythms continued: combinations

The previous examples utilize an eighth or sixteenth rhythm placed on one beat. However, what if you want to create (and play) denser phrases? Well, let's combine Chapter 6's hi-hat fragment approach within our quarter-note triplet exercises. I have relisted the previous two hi-hat keys below:

combination key

Add the hi-hat fragment
where the quarter note falls

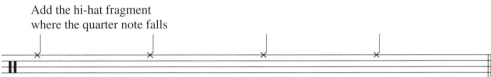

hi-hat fragments

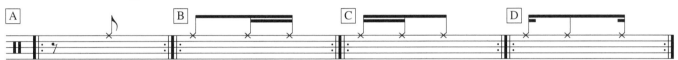

After utilizing the combination methods on the previous pages, here is a brief demonstration on creating interesting (and more dense) rhythmic hi-hat variations.

CD TRACK 74

Upon completing a mixed rhythm combination method, apply the following steps:

1. Using the first combination example on page 60, locate the quarter-note hi-hat:

2. Next, choose a hi-hat fragment from the chart above. In this case, I'll choose letter D.

3. Finally, place the hi-hat fragment within the quarter-note hi-hat:

BACKING MATERIAL : APPLYING WHAT YOU HAVE LEARNED

Now that you are comfortable with many of the previous methods, let's utilize these quarter-note triplet and mixed phrases alongside music. As such, feel free to insert your favorite fragments and phrases within the chart below.

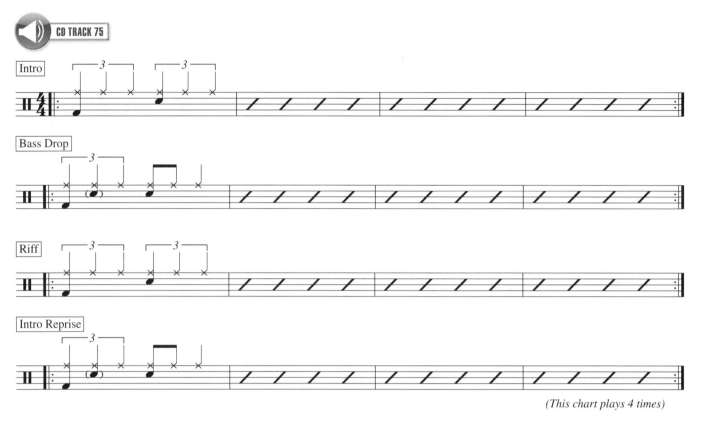

(This chart plays 4 times)

ADDITIONAL PRACTICE METHOD FOR ALL CHAPTERS: SNARE FILLS AND DECAYS (SIMULATED REVERB TRAILS)

Dubstep producers use snare fills with long reverb decays, which is borrowed from the sound-system Jamaican dub culture. To review, these snare fills are sent through various tape echoes (or their digital simulated counterparts), and the signals often degenerate in tone. As a result, each individual repeat (echo) either becomes progressively brighter or darker, effectively raising or lowering the pitch of the snare drum.

From a drummer's standpoint, these snare fills are quite strange because:

- They occur on an odd place within the beat (from what drummers are commonly used to). For example, instead of playing a fill directly on a beat (beats one, two, three, or four), this technique usually starts on the "e" or "ah" of a beat.
- Most dubstep tracks are programmed, so the fill is also played within a quarter- or eighth-note hi-hat pattern, too.
- Tom fills are not usually used within this style.
- Multiple snare drums must be utilized in order to recreate the pitch variations within these fill archetypes.

SETUP: TWO ADDITIONAL SNARE DRUMS

In order to get the most out of this section, I suggest adding two auxiliary snare drums to your acoustic drum setup. One should be tuned higher than your current snare and placed to the left of your main snare drum. The other should be tuned lower than your current snare and placed in a normal floor tom location. For example:

The snare setup is notated like this:

Main Snare   Left Auxiliary Snare   Right Auxiliary Snare
               Tuned High   Tuned Low

COMMON FILLS

With these facts in mind, I have listed some common fill-fragment rhythms for your review.

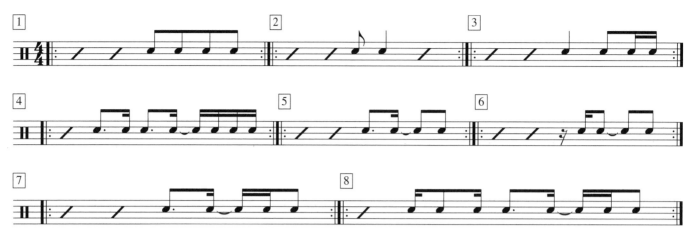

adding a quarter-note hi-hat

If you played each of these fragments with a quarter-note hi-hat, they would be played as follows:

CD TRACK 76

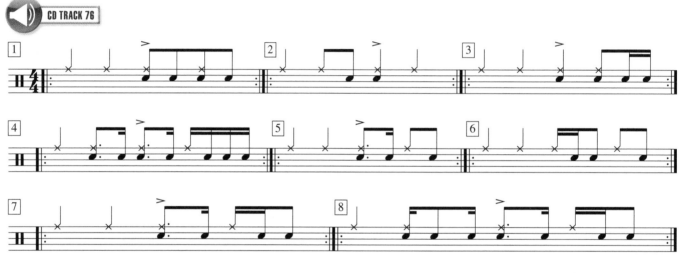

By choosing fragment No. 1 and by adding the kick drum on beat one, it would be played like this:

CD TRACK 77

However, if you chose fragment No. 7, it would be played as follows:

adding an eighth–note hi–hat

If you played each of these fragments alongside an eighth-note hi-hat, they would be played as follows:

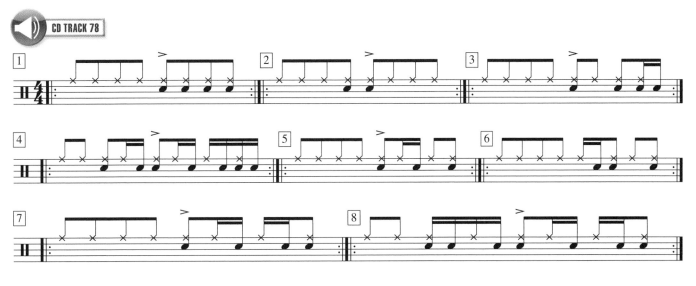

Again, by choosing fragment No. 1 and adding the kick drum on beat one, it would be played like this:

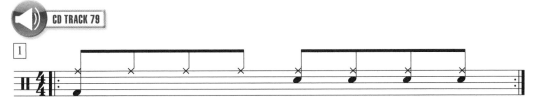

However, if you chose fragment No. 7, it would be played as follows:

ADDING THE PITCH VARIATIONS

As we discussed earlier, these fills either rise or descend in pitch. As we cannot perform pitch bends on an acoustic kit, let's use the aforementioned three snare drum setup to our advantage.

an ascending pitched fill

With this in mind, let's employ No. 1 from the quarter-note demonstration and move the last three eighth notes to the high-tuned snare like this:

If we add eighth notes to this pattern and melodic motion, it will be played as follows:

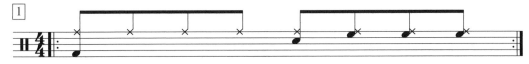

a descending pitched fill

In contrast to the last examples, let's employ No. 7 from the quarter-note demonstration and move the last three snare articulations to the low snare, like this:

Again, if we add eighth notes to this pattern and melodic motion, it will be played as follows:

FILL PRACTICE METHOD

Once you have mastered any one of the fill exercises, pick any groove in the previous chapters and practice your fills within the following fill practice method. In this exercise, you will play three bars of time and then your selected fill in measure 4. For example:

Insert fill measure here:

For the sake of this familiarity, let's choose fill No. 7 alongside an eighth-note hi-hat and descending snare pattern. Thus, if we placed it into this practice method, it would be played as follows:

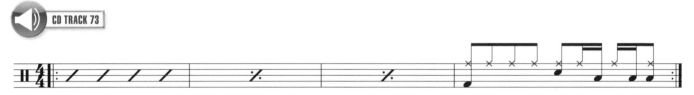

However, if you chose fill No. 1 with the quarter-note hi-hat and ascending snare pattern, it would be played like this:

Now that you understand these fill rhythms, melodic motions, and fill practice methods, feel free to experiment with them alongside the various grooves, play-alongs, and practice media within each of the previous chapters.

Chapter 8: Transcriptions

Now that you have reviewed each chapter in detail, let's examine some influential and real-world dubstep grooves. The following transcriptions are not meant to be an all-inclusive list, but rather a good overview (and entrance point) into the genre. Thus, I've included many early innovators alongside many of today's more pop-infused tracks.

Furthermore, as you are reading through each groove example, please keep in mind that the notated (written) grooves are the basic structure of what to play. It would be quite impossible to notate every little "sound" or synthetic texture within a dubstep groove. Therefore (just like chart reading), it is open to interpretation.

THE INNOVATORS

In this section, I have transcribed many of the early forefathers and innovators of the dubstep style. These grooves feature many of dubstep's hallmark rigid half-time beats and syncopated hi-hats. You'll also notice that each producer is very playful with sonic textures as well. Therefore (and where appropriate), I've done my best to notate these additional sounds.

digital mystikz

Earth a Run Red

Quarter note = 139 bpm

This track is seriously influenced by Jamaican dub and features an extremely heavy groove. There are also hi-hat accents notated on beats two and four, which is actually a white-noise type of sound. In addition (and as the track progresses), the groove expands with many hi-hat variations and subtle kick drum additions. I've notated the main pattern for you below:

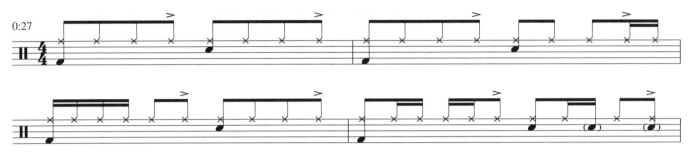

Anti War Dub

Half note = 140 bpm

This Digital Mystikz track has a heavy two feel, and the second stave features a bongo-esque sound that you could voice on a second snare, bongo, conga, or other percussion voice.

benga

Killer Step

Quarter note = 139 bpm

In this example, Benga utilizes multiple hi-hat parts alongside a heavy half-note kick and snare pattern. The lower stave features a very quiet second kick drum and synth bass part.

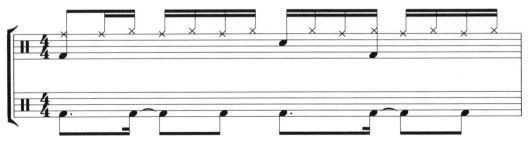

I Will Never Change

Quarter note = 140 bpm

In this groove, Benga employs a very heavy and dub-like kick and snare sound. In addition, the hi-hat is substituted for an electronic ride cymbal. Therefore (when playing this groove), you should use a high pitched (and washy) ride cymbal.

burial

Wounder

Quarter note = 141 bpm

This 8-bar phrase is quite interesting—yet repetitive. The lower stave features a very quiet (and distant sounding) second cross-stick snare drum part.

coki

Mood Dub

Quarter note = 136 bpm

This cut is very repetitive, but sonically diverse. In both bars, the "&" of beat two features an extremely powerful synthetic clap. The last eighth in bar two also employs a dry-staccato clap.

kode9

Black Sun

Quarter note = 130 bpm

This cyclical groove features cross-stick and snare articulations within each measure.

Magnetic City

Quarter note = 141 bpm

Kode9 keeps the same structure throughout this groove, while intermittently adding hi-hat and snare fills that decay into the background.

n–type

Early Door Jaw

Quarter note = 140 bpm

Multiple sounds are used within the Intro. These include three hi-hat sounds and two distortion variants. A long gated white-noise distortion is used on beat three, which is layered with the snare drum. There is also a scrape-like distortion on beat two, measure one, and on the "&" of beat four in measure two. These devices continue during the bass drop, but the hi-hat remains on one pitch and employs eighth notes throughout.

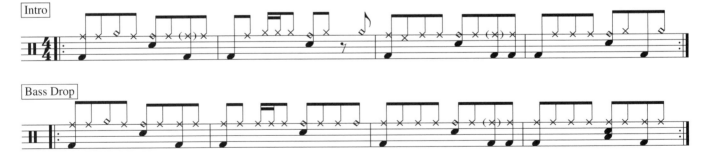

Tolerance

Quarter note = 139 bpm

In this instance, N-Type maintains the same kick and snare structure, while employing additional hi-hat rhythms. At 4:22, a percussion bongo-type sound is added on top of the established groove (from 4:02).

skream

Midnight Request Line

Quarter note = 140 bpm

Skream employs rests within the Intro, which are featured alongside wide clap sounds and playful dropouts (during bars five and six). In the riff sections, the "ah" of beat 3 is placed on a second synthetic 808-inspired kick sound, and in the second riff section, a second hi-hat is added on beats three and four. These are immensely straight and robotic (compared to the rest of the groove).

Rutten

Quarter note = 140 bpm

Skream programs the intro drums in a very hip-hop like manner. The "ah" of beat four is neither straight nor swung, but rather in the cracks of each feel. Thus (and in order to absorb this groove), you must listen to this track! During the bass drop, the semi-shuffled dotted eighth/sixteenth-note fragment is moved to beat three. This is the perfect juxtaposition to the straight eighth notes on beat four.

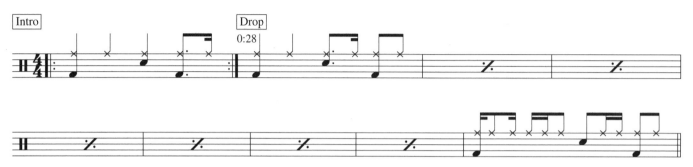

POP-INFUSED TRACKS

In this section, I have transcribed some recent pop-infused tracks. These grooves feature many of dub-step's hallmark rigid half-time beats and syncopated hi-hats alongside popular mainstream verses, choruses, and hooks.

12th planet, juakali

Reasons (Dr. P Remix)

Quarter note = 141 bpm

This vocal composition features four distinct sections and groove variations. Sonically, fat kicks are used alongside wide clap samples. A ride cymbal is employed during the riff sections, too.

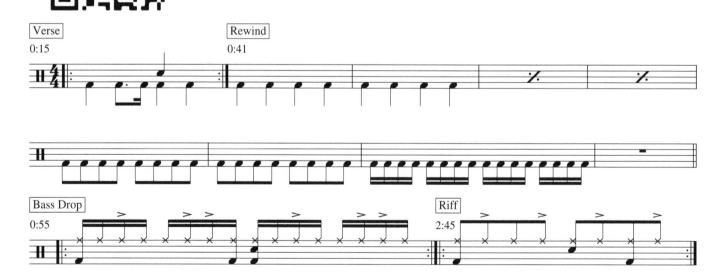

the bug, warrior queen

Poison Dart

Quarter note = 143 bpm

This static groove has a winding hi-hat pattern and a snare decay fill on beat three of each bar. In addition, the snare pitches upward in bar 1 and downward in bar 2 as follows (the second stave):

pitched up
snare

pitched down
snare

girl unit

Wut

Quarter note = 140 bpm

This vocal pop track utilizes devices from all the previous chapters, including eighth- and sixteenth-note grooves, which are combined alongside quarter-note triplet patterns. At 3:40, an eighth-note triplet hi-hat is played against the straight eighth- and sixteenth-note kick and snare pattern (from the main vocal section).

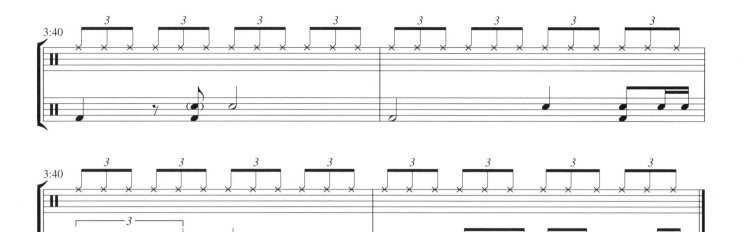

joy orbison

Hyph Mngo

Half note = 143 bpm

This groove borrows heavily from house and dance music. The main groove has an extremely syncopated hi-hat, and the snare fill on bar four (stave two) descends in pitch. A tambourine plays a static pattern throughout as well.

katy b

Katy on a Mission

Quarter note = 138 bpm

This vocal pop tune utilizes two hi-hat pitches and employs the Skream-like dotted eighth- and sixteenth-note fragment from *Rutten* on beat four (not straight or swung; but in between both feels). The hi-hat on beat four should be played as a long (extended) slightly open note as well.

la roux

In for the Kill (Skream's Let's Get Ravey Remix)

Quarter note = 138 bpm

In this tune, Skream employs a static groove alongside a wide-gated snare and punchy kick drum. The groove is very reminiscent of early Digital Mystikz tracks, which is the perfect juxtaposition to the clean vocal and synth-pop instrumentation present in the mix.

skrillex

Scary Monsters and Nice Sprites

Quarter note = 141

Although most purists may consider this brostep, it did make U.S. listeners aware of the dubstep genre. Thus it deserves special mention here. The intro and bass drop grooves are very traditional with their eighth-note hi-hat, wide-gated snare, and slightly syncopated kick drum patterns. However, the sixteenth note on the "ah" of beat two within the bass drop is also neither straight nor swung. At 2:52 (the Intro reprise), the hi-hats alternate pitches and become busier as well.

HAL·LEONARD DRUM PLAY-ALONG™

Play your favorite songs quickly and easily with the *Drum Play-Along*™ series. Just follow the drum notation, listen to the CD to hear how the drums should sound, then play along using the separate backing tracks. The lyrics are also included for quick reference. The audio CD is playable on any CD player. For PC and Mac computer users, the CD is enhanced so you can adjust the recording to any tempo without changing the pitch!

1. Pop/Rock
Hurts So Good • Message in a Bottle • No Reply at All • Owner of a Lonely Heart • Peg • Rosanna • Separate Ways (Worlds Apart) • Swingtown.
00699742 Book/CD Pack $12.95

2. Classic Rock
Barracuda • Come Together • Mississippi Queen • Radar Love • Space Truckin' • Walk This Way • White Room • Won't Get Fooled Again.
00699741 Book/CD Pack $12.95

3. Hard Rock
Bark at the Moon • Detroit Rock City • Living After Midnight • Panama • Rock You like a Hurricane • Run to the Hills • Smoke on the Water • War Pigs (Interpolating Luke's Wall).
00699743 Book/CD Pack $12.95

4. Modern Rock
Chop Suey! • Duality • Here to Stay • Judith • Nice to Know You • Nookie • One Step Closer • Whatever.
00699744 Book/CD Pack $12.95

5. Funk
Cissy Strut • Cold Sweat, Part 1 • Fight the Power, Part 1 • Flashlight • Pick Up the Pieces • Shining Star • Soul Vaccination • Superstition.
00699745 Book/CD Pack $14.99

6. '90s Rock
Alive • Been Caught Stealing • Cherub Rock • Give It Away • I'll Stick Around • Killing in the Name • Shine • Smells Like Teen Spirit.
00699746 Book/CD Pack $14.99

7. Punk Rock
All the Small Things • Brain Stew (The Godzilla Remix) • Buddy Holly • Dirty Little Secret • Fat Lip • Flavor of the Weak • Lifestyles of the Rich and Famous • Self Esteem.
00699747 Book/CD Pack $14.99

8. '80s Rock
Cult of Personality • Heaven's on Fire • Rock of Ages • Shake Me • Smokin' in the Boys Room • Talk Dirty to Me • We're Not Gonna Take It • You Give Love a Bad Name.
00699832 Book/CD Pack $12.95

9. Big Band
Christopher Columbus • Corner Pocket • Flying Home • In the Mood • Opus One • Stompin' at the Savoy • Take the "A" Train • Woodchopper's Ball.
00699833 Book/CD Pack $12.99

10. blink-182
Adam's Song • All the Small Things • Dammit • Feeling This • Man Overboard • The Rock Show • Stay Together for the Kids • What's My Age Again?
00699834 Book/CD Pack $14.95

11. Jimi Hendrix Experience: Smash Hits
All Along the Watchtower • Can You See Me? • Crosstown Traffic • Fire • Foxey Lady • Hey Joe • Manic Depression • Purple Haze • Red House • Remember • Stone Free • The Wind Cries Mary.
00699835 Book/CD Pack $16.95

12. The Police
Can't Stand Losing You • De Do Do Do, De Da Da Da • Don't Stand So Close to Me • Every Breath You Take • Every Little Thing She Does Is Magic • Spirits in the Material World • Synchronicity II • Walking on the Moon.
00700268 Book/CD Pack $14.99

13. Steely Dan
Deacon Blues • Do It Again • FM • Hey Nineteen • Josie • My Old School • Reeling in the Years.
00700202 Book/CD Pack $16.99

14. The Doors
Break on Through to the Other Side • Hello, I Love You (Won't You Tell Me Your Name?) • L.A. Woman • Light My Fire • Love Me Two Times • People Are Strange • Riders on the Storm • Roadhouse Blues.
00699887 Book/CD Pack $14.95

15. Lennon & McCartney
Back in the U.S.S.R. • Day Tripper • Drive My Car • Get Back • A Hard Day's Night • Paperback Writer • Revolution • Ticket to Ride.
00700271 Book/CD Pack $14.99

17. Nirvana
About a Girl • All Apologies • Come As You Are • Dumb • Heart Shaped Box • In Bloom • Lithium • Smells like Teen Spirit.
00700273 Book/CD Pack $14.95

18. Motown
Ain't Too Proud to Beg • Dancing in the Street • Get Ready • How Sweet It Is (To Be Loved by You) • I Can't Help Myself (Sugar Pie, Honey Bunch) • Sir Duke • Stop! in the Name of Love • You've Really Got a Hold on Me.
00700274 Book/CD Pack $12.99

19. Rock Band: Modern Rock Edition
Are You Gonna Be My Girl • Black Hole Sun • Creep • Dani California • In Bloom • Learn to Fly • Say It Ain't So • When You Were Young.
00700707 Book/CD Pack $14.95

20. Rock Band: Classic Rock Edition
Ballroom Blitz • Detroit Rock City • Don't Fear the Reaper • Gimme Shelter • Highway Star • Mississippi Queen • Suffragette City • Train Kept A-Rollin'.
00700708 Book/CD Pack $14.95

21. Weezer
Beverly Hills • Buddy Holly • Dope Nose • Hash Pipe • My Name Is Jonas • Pork and Beans • Say It Ain't So • Undone – The Sweater Song.
00700959 Book/CD Pack $14.99

22. Black Sabbath
Children of the Grave • Iron Man • N.I.B. • Paranoid • Sabbath, Bloody Sabbath • Sweet Leaf • War Pigs (Interpolating Luke's Wall).
00701190 Book/CD Pack $16.99

23. The Who
Baba O'Riley • Bargain • Behind Blue Eyes • The Kids Are Alright • Long Live Rock • Pinball Wizard • The Seeker • Won't Get Fooled Again.
00701191 Book/CD Pack $16.99

24. Pink Floyd – Dark Side of the Moon
Any Colour You Like • Brain Damage • Breathe • Eclipse • Money • Time • Us and Them.
00701612 Book/CD Pack $14.99

25. Bob Marley
Could You Be Loved • Get Up Stand Up • I Shot the Sheriff • Is This Love • Jamming • No Woman No Cry • Stir It Up • Three Little Birds • Waiting in Vain.
00701703 Book/CD Pack $14.99

26. Aerosmith
Back in the Saddle • Draw the Line • Dream On • Last Child • Mama Kin • Same Old Song and Dance • Sweet Emotion • Walk This Way.
00701887 Book/CD Pack $14.99

27. Modern Worship
Beautiful One • Days of Elijah • Hear Our Praises • Holy Is the Lord • How Great Is Our God • I Give You My Heart • Worthy Is the Lamb • You Are Holy (Prince of Peace).
00701921 Book/CD Pack $12.99

28. Avenged Sevenfold
Afterlife • Almost Easy • Bat Country • Beast and the Harlot • Nightmare • Scream • Unholy Confessions.
00702388 Book/CD Pack $17.99

31. Red Hot Chili Peppers
The Adventures of Rain Dance Maggie • By the Way • Californication • Can't Stop • Dani California • Scar Tissue • Suck My Kiss • Tell Me Baby • Under the Bridge.
00702992 Book/CD Pack $19.99

32. Songs for Beginners
Another One Bites the Dust • Billie Jean • Green River • Helter Skelter • I Won't Back Down • Living After Midnight • The Reason • 21 Guns.
00704204 Book/CD Pack $14.99

HAL·LEONARD®
CORPORATION
7777 W. BLUEMOUND RD. P.O. BOX 13819 MILWAUKEE, WI 53213

Visit Hal Leonard Online at
www.halleonard.com

0913

Prices, contents and availability subject to change without notice and may vary outside the US.